NO TIME FOR PATIENCE

NO TIME FOR PATIENCE

My Road from Kaunas to Jerusalem

A Memoir of a Holocaust Survivor

Zev Birger

Foreword by Shimon Peres

Newmarket Press New York

FIRST ENGLISH-LANGUAGE EDITION
10   9   8   7   6   5   4   3   2   1

Library of Congress Cataloging-in-Publication Data:
Birger, Zev.
  [Keine Zeit fur Geduld. English]
  No time for patience: my road from Kaunas to Jerusalem :
a memoir of a Holocaust survivor/Zev Birger; foreword by
Shimon Peres.
    p. cm.
  ISBN 1-55704-386-8 (hc)
   1. Birger, Zev, 1926–   .   2. Jews— Lithuania— Kaunas
Biography.   3. Holocaust, Jewish (1939–1945)
Lithuania — Kaunas Personal narratives.   4. Kaunas
(Lithuania) Biography.   5. Holocaust survivors — Israel
Biography.   I. Title
DS135.L53B573   1999
940.53' 18' 092— dc21   99-3022
  [B]   CIP

Quantity Purchases
Companies, professional groups, clubs, and other organizations
may qualify for special terms when ordering quantities of this title.
For information, write Special Sales, Newmarket Press, 18 East
48th Street, New York, NY 10017, call (212) 832-3575, or fax
(212) 832-3629.

Designed by Tania Garcia

Manufactured in the United States of America.

Contents

FOREWORD

by Shimon Peres

The title of the book — No Time for Patience — is a very fitting one, reflecting the approach Zev Birger has adopted to his public work, his strong sense of having to make up for "lost" time, and his desire to take on as many tasks as possible. Zev's achievements and the range of enterprises he has headed or played a part in developing could easily provide the substance for several lifetimes of public service.

During Israel's early years, Zev was among the founders of the Tax and Excise Department. He helped formulate Israel's indirect taxation system, and prepared the organizational infrastructure for the department. During the Six Day War (1967), Zev was asked to reorganize the Ministry of Industry. In this capacity, he worked energetically to promote industry in Israel, placing particular emphasis on the development of light industry. His personal interest in languages, literature, and the theater led him to assist the fledgling movie industry in Israel, as well as the fields of publishing and design.

Zev's life took another turn when the former mayor of Jerusalem, Teddy Kollek, asked him to take on a number of positions. Zev worked alongside Kollek for many years, and Kollek's farsighted vision of the status of Jerusalem as Israel's capital enabled Zev to work in a wide range of fields, implementing numerous projects that furthered the culture, tourism, and economic life of the city.

During all the time he was working in administrative positions, Zev's true love was books. After being appointed director of the Jerusalem Fairs and Conventions Bureau, which was established to manage the International Book Fair, Zev encouraged and initiated congresses and international fairs in the capital, as well as taking part in numerous activities to promote culture and tourism there. The Jerusalem International Judaica Fair is an excellent example of his endeavors.

Under Zev's management, the Jerusalem Book Fair has become one of the largest and most important book fairs in the world. By adding a series of conventions and events, Zev enhanced the fair's prestige and gained international recognition. His unique personality and his position as director of the International Jerusalem Book Fair has enabled him to serve as an ambassador for Israel and Jerusalem in the world of international publishing.

Zev's story is one that must be told. Despite living through the Nazi hell, Zev never lost his faith in humanity or in human culture and creativity. With limitless optimism, he devoted his energy to working seriously and lovingly to strengthen the State of Israel. For Zev, the only way for the Jewish people to overcome the disasters of the past was to build a new life — a life of freedom and creativity.

Zev embodies a combination of culture, optimism, and friendship that has made him a veritable institution in the life of Jerusalem.

ACKNOWLEDGMENTS

I would like to express my most heartfelt thanks to the many friends, editors, and publishers who took the initiative to set this project in motion. I would especially like to thank Dr. Petra Eggers, who simply forced me to cooperate with her in this project. I also owe a debt of gratitude to Christoph Buchwald and his colleagues at Luchterhand, as well as the Hoffman Agency, C. H. Beck Verlag, Berlin Verlag, Campus Verlag, Carl Hanser Verlag, Econ Verlag, Eggers & Landwehr KG, S. Fisher Verlag, Liepman AG, Piper Verlag, Rowohlt Verlag, and Verlagsgruppe Bertelsmann, all of whom took the initiative and dedicated this book to me and published it in Germany.

I feel deeply grateful to a friend who became my publisher, Esther Margolis. Thanks to her encouragement and support, and her colleagues and staff, along with editor Theresa Burns, the English edition of this book came into being. It is because of them that my sons and grandchildren will be able to read my story and, as a result, understand and appreciate their roots.

My warmest thanks to Michele and Dan Sagir for their translation into English, which they did with much love and dedication.

And last but not least, I am deeply obligated and grateful to my wife, Trudi, who created a warm and loving home for our family and our sons' families, and without whose moral support it would have been impossible to revive my memories and recount them.

AUTHOR'S NOTE

I was able to write this book by keeping my feelings and emotions in check and making myself detached from the story. I am sorry that this was the case, that I was unable to open up my heart and express my innermost feelings. There are many untold incidents still locked inside of me, and I hope there will come a day when I will find the inner strength to recount them, too.

I

BACK TO DACHAU

It was a cold day, April 27, 1995, when I attended the memorial service for the Fiftieth Anniversary of the Liberation of the Prisoners of Kaufering Concentration Camp. But the cold was a reflection of more than Germany's crisp spring weather. The winds of the past do not always blow lightly; they can also resurface as icy gusts, transformed into such by memory.

I looked over at my three sons, Doron, Oded, and Gil, and wondered what they were thinking. For I had finally broken my silence after many years, and begun to speak about the atrocious past. During the speeches given at this memorial service in Landsberg for victims of Kaufering, the external camp of Dachau concentration camp, I gave free rein to my thoughts and pondered the two central questions of my life: Why had I kept silent for so long, and why was I breaking the silence now?

First, why had I kept silent? This question is easier to answer than the second. When the war ended, I decided to keep silent after I asked myself, If someone were to come to you and tell you that they had gone through such things, wouldn't you think they were hopelessly exaggerating? Wouldn't you think it unfathomable that a human being could have been subjected to such horrendous experiences and survived?

At the time, I did not want anyone to think that I was exaggerating, thereby compromising the memory of the dead. I did not want to seem melodramatic, as if I were blowing things up out of proportion. For this reason I did not even tell my sons about the horrible experiences in Lithuania and later in Germany. How can you give your children the joy of living and courage in life if at the same time you tell them about such inhumanity, such injustice, such atrocities? Isn't it better to remain silent? But during the Yom Kippur War, when in 1973 the Egyptians launched a surprise attack against Israel while the entire country was in the midst of its holiest holiday, there was a seemingly insignificant incident that caused me to change my attitude.

At the time, my eldest son, Doron, was serving in the air force, and the youngest was still at home. My middle son, Oded, who was serving in the armored corps, had just completed a course as tank commander. He was celebrating the successful end of training with some friends when the festivities came to an abrupt halt. The group was suddenly sent to Sinai, and the war broke out two days later. Oded had served only two days as commander in action when his tank was hit by a rocket. The fierce fighting that ensued demanded all the soldiers' strength.

After one especially difficult battle, Oded sent us a postcard from Sinai that read: "Dear parents, even if this war is terrible, please do not worry, we will win — there is no going back to Dachau."

These lines shocked me. If an eighteen-year-old — and my son in particular — felt like that, if for him the current struggle was not only a question of victory or surrender but also of Dachau, then I owed him my history, the history of his family and his grandparents, whom he had never known.

After the war I went together with my son to the Western Wall, also called the Wailing Wall, to commemorate his friends who had fallen during the Yom Kippur War. It was on this occasion that I told him for the first time about my past. But even this was not the event that made me decide to tell my whole story. That decision came about only on the trip to Kaufering, the external camp of Dachau, where we now stood. Nonetheless, during those moments at the Western Wall, it became clear to me that in surviving I had also been given the responsibility of telling about the events, to prevent them from recurring. The path that led from Kaunas, my childhood home, to Kaufering, and then on to a new life and family in Jerusalem, was a long one. The brief visit to Kaufering so many years later was the catalyst that forced me to confront my past, and it was in committing the memories to writing that my personal history came full circle.

2

CHILDHOOD

YEARS OF NORMALCY

My mother was born Fejga Zipora Kaplan in the small Lithuanian town of Kedainja. Her father was a very talented house painter, who worked with the Germans at the time of the occupation of Lithuania during World War I. My mother was fluent in German, since even as a small child she had assisted her father. But my grandfather was not just an ordinary painter; he also had an artistic bent, and now and then used to paint frescoes. He was a kind of freelance artistic painter. My mother's family had deeply embedded roots in the Jewish tradition, which also affected our family life to a certain extent.

As is the case in almost every Jewish family, our lives were very much influenced by my mother's personality. She had a very tender nature. No loud words were needed; she was able to restrain her children with her soft voice. I had a cousin, young Bella, who lived with us for a time and had the bad habit of slamming the doors loudly when leaving the house. This upset my mother very much and she wanted to "educate" her. But instead of shouting at her every time she slammed the door, my mother one day ran after my cousin through the entire city park that bordered on our home, and called to her: "Come back home, immediately! Come quickly!" My cousin was very frightened and wanted to know the reason, but my mother gave no answer, simply repeating her request, barely able to suppress her laughter when she saw my cousin's alarmed look. When they got back to the house, my cousin again asked what had happened. To which Fejga Birger simply answered: "Please shut the doors quietly."

My parents met in the early 1920s through a mutual acquaintance and soon got married. The home they created was very warm and full of love, where no quarrels or angry words were heard. I often used to wonder if I perhaps remembered only the pleasant aspects of our home life and simply blocked out the unpleasant ones. One tends, over time, to paint the past in rosy colors. But even after intensive reflection I cannot recall any loud scenes in my family.

On the contrary, our home was exceedingly harmonious. My parents held strong Zionist views, firmly believing in the need to establish a Jewish homeland in Palestine, but they nonetheless led a tradition-oriented life. We observed the Sabbath, visited the synagogue on the High Holidays, Rosh Hashanah and Yom Kippur, and ate kosher food. As a child I especially liked baking challah, the white plaited bread, for the

Sabbath. The loaves were baked in the enormous stove, which was the best place to sleep near during the winter. The kitchen was not a modern one, it consisted only of that open stove. I was allowed to assist my mother with the baking, and was given the "important" task of brushing egg yolk on the plaited loaves. When my mother lit the candles on the Sabbath and said the prayers, I felt especially proud, since I had contributed to the celebration of this day.

My mother had many relatives, among them an older sister. This sister was married and had two small daughters. But she was murdered by robbers during the Bolshevik riots that took place in the wake of the Russian Revolution in 1917. My mother, who even as a young girl had both feet firmly planted on the ground, drove to her sister's and simply took the two girls. And this as an unmarried woman! Years later we used to laugh when father told us how my mother, as the bride, brought two small girls with her under the canopy. I have never since met such a clever and capable woman, who radiated both warmth and an openhearted kindness.

My father, Pinchas Birger, was a very composed, tranquil man. So far-reaching was his social commitment that people used to say of him that he didn't know the meaning of property. Everything he had he gave to others. He was a construction engineer, which was quite an achievement for a Jewish citizen in Lithuania, given the widespread anti-Semitism in Eastern Europe, which made it at that time extremely difficult for a Jew to become part of the "intelligentsia."

My father was born in a small town in Lithuania, near the border with Lettland and Russia. The landscape there is very beautiful, with many small lakes, and for this reason the area is called Little Switzerland.

We lived in the center of the city of Kaunas, then capital of Lithuania because Vilnius, the historical capital, was under Polish rule. In those times Kaunas was a flourishing city with a large Jewish community, numbering around forty thousand.

Thanks to my father's occupation, my family belonged to the middle class — the bourgeoisie — and economically, our situation was not so bad. We were culturally and politically integrated but also observed some aspects of Jewish tradition. Though my father had a profession, all practical decisions at home were made by my mother: which schools the children would attend, what items should be purchased for the household, how money should be spent. Since my father built bridges, public buildings, schools, and other structures for the government in many different places, he spent a great deal of time on the road and frequently came home only on the weekends. But then he dedicated himself entirely to the family and looked after us devotedly. On summer vacations we often drove to different places where my father was working at the time. He was very sought-after in his profession — besides his other public-building jobs, he worked on large projects for the Lithuanian military, and was chosen by the government to take part in the construction of the large bridge at the main river crossing in Kaunas. The Lithuanian government decorated him for his years of service and excellent performance. Unfortunately, this did not help him later when the Russians, then the Germans, came to Kaunas.

During our vacations, when my small world was still ordered, we lived with the Lithuanian farmers and worked with the hired hands, going out to the fields with them to collect the hay and doing other tasks. For us children, it was always great fun, and we enjoyed life in the country very much. We lived with the land and the people, the big fields and the many lakes. For a long time, it seemed as if nothing could upset this harmony. On the farm we drank fresh milk still frothy from the milkmaid's bucket. Today this would be considered unhygienic, but in those days nobody thought twice about such things, and I am sure that the fresh cows milk did us no harm.

One event left a particular impression in my memory. It was summer and we were again staying as vacation guests with a family of Lithuanian farmers in a small village. There was a large forest that had to be crossed in order to reach the farm. One night we found ourselves traveling across the field in a coach in a terrible thunderstorm. We were scared out of our wits. Even the Lithuanian coachman could barely hide his fear. Suddenly, lightning hit a tree near us. We were terrified. Since then I have always been afraid of thunder and lightning. Still, these vacation memories are among the best I have, since they reflect the happy relations we had with Lithuanians then, in particular with the rural people.

My older brother was born in 1922. My parents named him Mordechai, but he was often just called Motke. I made my own appearance in 1926 and my parents gave me the name Wolf. My nickname was Wulik, a kind of Russian diminutive of the name. Although the most common language in Jewish Kaunas was Yiddish, we spoke a lot of Russian and German at home. In fact, a wild confusion of languages prevailed. Polish was added to the mix by our Polish housekeeper. Our nannies, who took care of us up until preschool, sometimes spoke Russian and sometimes German, so that my brother and I grew up multilingual, sometimes creating a real language cocktail. At home the conversations were mostly in Yiddish. My brother and I also spoke Hebrew between us, since this was the language of instruction at school. When my parents wrote letters, they were mainly in Yiddish, but some sentences were in German or Russian. We always subscribed to two or three newspapers in different languages: *The Jewish Voice,* as well as the most important newspaper in the Lithuanian language, the *Lietuvos Aidas,* and also a newspaper from Germany.

We grew used to the mix of languages in our house, since life there was a lot like a busy railway station. We almost always had friends visiting, guests or refugees. We had two extra guest rooms, which were off-limits to my brother and me; we were not allowed even to enter them. Guests often slept on our couch when all the beds were occupied. My parents were so welcoming and openhearted with guests that I can hardly recall a day when there weren't one or two young people staying with us, spending the night, or sharing a meal.

In those days many young people used to go to Kaunas to study or look for work, but they had no idea of where to spend the night. People who had to wait for their travel documents also found shelter with us. For example, a woman whom I met by chance many years later at an acquaintance's in America told me: "We came from a small town in Lithuania and had to wait for our papers, for the journey to America. This took a long time and we did not know where we should stay. Then someone advised us to go to Fejga Birger, who had an open house. I came to her with my three small children and was immediately received with open arms. We stayed there for almost two months, just like that. It was so taken for granted, and things were so wonderful in your house. Your mother took us to the railway station, where we left for New York. Never before had I experienced something like that. Only rarely in life does one encounter such warmth and such an open heart." My mother was indeed a special woman. Warmhearted, clever, talented, and down to earth.

Through our open house, we also began to understand the significance of the political developments in Germany. From 1933 on, we had many political refugees living with us, from Poland, from Germany, from all over Europe. My parents had definite Zionist leanings. What that meant was that we talked a lot about Palestine. We had a burning interest in everything that went on in Palestine at that time. Palestine, or "Eretz Israel"—the Land of Israel, as the Jews called it—was then part of the British Mandate, which controlled two rival national liberation movements: the Zionist movement of the Jews, and the Palestinian movement of the Arabs. When friends of ours emigrated to Palestine, when they made aliyah (literally, "ascended to the land"), they were always invited to visit us, and the subject was discussed at great length.

My parents were close to the liberal Zionist associations, but unfortunately had no real emigration plans. Zionism for them was less a political issue and more a matter of commitment, of contact with Israel. And I would never have taken a trip anywhere, let alone emigrated, without my parents. The issue became relevant in our house for the first time in 1939, when the clouds of war spread over Europe, even before the invasion of the Russians. But it was too late. In spite of their basic Zionist orientation, my parents did not seriously contemplate a move to Palestine. Until then, we had led a very calm life. Like so many others, we simply refused to believe that the Germans could invade Lithuania. I had a very happy and serene youth, a warm home, and many friends. Somehow, everything seemed planned for me in advance: I went to school, then would have gone to the university, and eventually would have emigrated to Palestine. My elder brother would have followed in our father's footsteps and studied engineering, and I, the younger, could perhaps have become a doctor. Like a mosaic, all the pieces were supposed to fit into place. Who would have thought that the small stones would suddenly be wrenched from the mosaic, hurled in all directions, and crushed underfoot?

Since we lived in the city center, our house was very near the municipal theater, which probably helped contribute to my love of the musical arts. There were two apartments in our house, ours and that of a Jewish family from Germany. We also had a backyard and a beautiful garden that bordered the Kaunas City Park. Many of my favorite childhood memories are connected to this garden. We played for hours among the trees. We performed our first experiments as gardeners and planted strawberries. In the middle of the garden was a tiny romantic summer house that would later, after the Russian invasion, take on special significance in my life.

The proximity to the city park granted me the best of both worlds as a child: I could enjoy the bustling excitement of city life; but there was also a little corner of nature where I could run around wild, and where we could play sports. There was a large café — the Konrad Café — in the city park where almost every afternoon a band used to play and the café-goers would dance. The most popular dances of the day were the waltz, the tango, the English waltz, and sometimes the Charleston. As children, we had great fun watching the young couples dancing. Since the café bordered directly on our garden, we used to make spy-holes in the wall, in order to find out exactly who came with whom and who danced with whom. Naturally we were a nuisance to the café patrons. Even today, I can see us standing there in our breeches watching through the holes and from time to time throwing small paper balls at the dancing couples.

Another social attraction close to our house was the State Opera. Even as a toddler I used to go at least once a week. Various operas were staged there — from *Carmen* to *Rigoletto* to *La Traviata*. Since the people in the box office knew me well and wanted to enhance my education, I was often able to attend the show without a ticket. Or I would wangle my way inside and sneak over to the standing-room area in the upper galleries. In this way, I saw all the great operas and ballets several times. I can recall in particular one delightful perform-ance — *Madama Butterfly* — which I got to enjoy even though there were no tickets left.

Sometimes my friends would take bets on who could sing more arias. I liked *Traviata* the best, and knew many arias by heart. It must have sound-ed very funny to the adults to hear such small voices singing the world's greatest arias! I also greatly appreciated Mephisto from *Faust,* when the famous bass Chaliapin came to our theater to sing the role. He was simply wonderful, and to this day I can recall with crystal clarity the deep, malevolent laughter of Mephisto.

The Jewish community in Kaunas was large, and community life in the city was very lively. There was a Jewish hospital, a Jewish bank, and other Jewish establishments. Many Jewish citizens were politically active, but in contrast to Jews living in Germany or Austria, where participation in the country's national culture led inevitably to identification with the local society and to assimilation, we had an independent Jewish life. Social contacts with non-Jews were rare. The only exceptions were the meetings my father held with his non-Jewish engineering colleagues and the Lithuanian farmers with whom we spent our vacations.

For me it would have been unthinkable to have a non-Jewish girlfriend or to marry a non-Jewish woman. Mixed marriages were an exception in Jewish circles. One didn't necessarily "sit Shiva," in formal mourning, but it was clear that such a marriage would have been a serious blow for a family. Our family was no different.

Almost all our friends were Jews, and most of them also belonged to the intelligentsia, which in those days consisted of a very small sector of the population. Lithuanian culture and literature were still poor — Lithuania was a young country, liberated only after the Russian Revolution at the end of World War I. After centuries of oppression and exploitation at the hands of the Russian czars, they were left with nothing but their political independence. Lithuania was a farmer's land, an agricultural country, whose population lived on butter and pork and the export of geese.

Relative to their percentage of the population, Jews made up a large part of the country's intelligentsia. They generally had a very high level of education and showed a lively interest in art and culture — they were avid opera lovers and ballet-goers. It was an open, heterogeneous society, which nevertheless was and remained Jewish, and showed almost no tendency to assimilate.

In addition, many Jews were politically active and shared the Zionist conviction that the Jews must live in their own land. Most of them, and in particular the younger generation, were waiting to go to Palestine and build the land. After the hard times faced under the Russian czars and in the often seemingly fruitless emancipation efforts, they hoped only for a better future and shifted their interest from emancipation to Zionism and state independence in Palestine. Those who initially promoted these efforts were from the cities, in particular Kaunas, where the Jewish population was especially Zionist oriented.

Jews of lower socioeconomic standing had socialist leanings, but not due to any ideological conviction. They wanted social justice, and the only non-Jewish option that offered itself was communism. Among the intelligentsia a minority were also close to the communist idea. They combined ideology with social conviction. In this way, the Jewish community reflected the tendencies of Lithuanian society in general, in which there was a minority that tended toward communism.

It is no wonder that there were hardly any encounters between Lithuanians, a largely anti-Semitic society, and the Jewish population. There were, of course, Lithuanian intellectuals who had not been infected by the widespread prejudice, but anti-Semitism was prevalent in day-to-day life. There were frequent riots by Lithuanian youth, directed in particular against Jewish students, and my brother and I were often involved in fights. We would be walking on the street and suddenly someone would shout "Zydas!" (Jew), and strike us. Depending on the circumstances, one had two options: run away or return the blow.

Very early on, while still in the lower grades, we prepared ourselves for such fights and trained ourselves in self-defense. Whenever possible, we walked in groups of at least two or three. Our strategy was to avoid being taken by surprise, and we were fairly effective. Eventually word got out that it was not pleasant business to quarrel with the students with the uniform and red caps from the Hebrew high school. I also had an advantage in that my brother was an excellent, well-trained athlete and a good protector. He was considered one of the toughest of our group, and taught our attackers the meaning of fear.

Unlike in Germany — where anti-Semitism was fostered by the government and fell on fertile soil — anti-Semitism in Lithuania was not of a political or media-based nature. No negative attitude prevailed in Lithuanian official circles, and the government was truly liberal toward the Jewish minority. But the Lithuanian citizens themselves were very nationalistic, and anti-Semitism was widespread, especially in the lower classes where only a small number were liberals.

Several Jews were active in the government and the Sejim, or parliament, but social contacts between them and the Lithuanians, if they existed at all, occurred only in the higher echelons and not with the country folk. Even within the rural population, Jews had no contacts with the Lithuanians; a kind of religiously motivated anti-Semitism prevailed, and contacts between the city and the countryside were very rare. At the university there was a quota system for Jewish students; my brother could study engineering only because he had especially good grades and because our father received a medal from the Lithuanian government for his construction of the city's major bridge and railway crossing.

I used to talk about the Lithuanians' anti-Semitism at length, particularly with my cousin Bella, who had lived with us since childhood. She was like a sister to me, and to this day I maintain very close contact with her three sons. The eldest is head of a hospital in New York, the second a professor of medicine in Jerusalem, and the youngest a psychiatrist in New York. So, as far as medical treatment goes, I am well looked after. I often think about how I used to joke with her, saying: "Both of us are at the same level: You are in the first year of university, and I am in the first grade of elementary school."

Bella was a bookworm, and passed this passion on to me. From my childhood I got used to reading everything that came my way. On several occasions this resulted in an argument with my parents when they saw that the light in my room was on until all hours. I used to turn it off and continue reading under the blanket, with the help of a flashlight. I was often engrossed in a book for the entire day, paying no attention to the outside world. At thirteen I started reading Nietzsche and discussing him with Bella. My teachers often asked me to talk about my reading. I read books in Hebrew, which I learned at school, and Lithuanian. I could also speak Russian and German, but it was too difficult to read literature in these languages. I was hopelessly in love with books, in particular with history books and historical novels. Kings, political intrigues, the Middle Ages, and the Romans were my favorite subjects. Past worlds fascinated me. My imagination embellished the stories further and enriched my life even more. Reading was also a means of shutting out the world around me, with its increasingly unpleasant events.

Bella encouraged this passion by supplying me with enormous quantities of reading material. We were always immersed in a conversation about some book or other. Bella had a considerable influence on my intellectual development and political orientation. She was highly intelligent and her thinking was well ahead of her time. She initiated numerous discussions at home — about the right of the individual in society, the political independence of peoples and nations, social problems, revolution, and much more. Many of her politically active young friends were regular visitors in our home, and the noise of heated debate filled our living room. Our talks revolved around the great problems of humanity, which we felt certain were unresolvable.

Bella was a very good student, passing all university tests summa cum laude, and when she graduated she became a literature and language teacher in the Jewish-Lithuanian high school. It was Bella who taught me the Latin and Hebrew alphabets before my first day of school. In 1939 she married a refugee from Nuremberg, a yeshiva student named Leo Adler, who escaped to Lithuania with his entire yeshiva. He was ordained as a rabbi in Lithuania. His group wanted to travel to Shanghai, and from there emigrate to the United States. But at the time, one had to endure the difficulties of a journey through Russia in order to reach Shanghai. Bella followed Leo and got stuck in Moscow when the war broke out. Her eldest son was born there, and later on she was sent together with him to Siberia. There was no milk in the work camp where she and her baby were sent, and to this day I don't know how she managed to survive with her baby under those conditions. After the liberation she finally met up with her husband, and the couple built their life in New York, far away — at least geographically — from all the horrible events that were taking place in Europe. Still, after several years they returned to Europe, and Leo was appointed chief rabbi of Basel in 1955, a position he held until he passed away in 1978.

One of the ways Bella demonstrated her sense of humor was by preparing a special surprise for my bar mitzvah — a surprise that would make us the talk of the town for several days. Like all Jewish boys at the age of thirteen, I prepared for my bar mitzvah, the acceptance of new members by the community and the "new man's" first public reading of the Torah. With the bar mitzvah — which, literally translated, means "son of the [divine] law" — one is obligated to accept all the commandments and to be responsible for one's own actions. For this reason, the boy's father also says a prayer on this occasion, in which he divests himself of any responsibility for his son's wrongdoing. According to Jewish tradition, this undertaking of the Law is eternal and irreversible, similar to the obligation of a son toward his father, which is also not to be broken. The first duty to perform is the reading of "Hear, O Israel" in the evening prayer.

The second duty is the wearing of phylacteries (leather boxes containing scriptural passages worn on the left arm and the head during morning prayers, also called tefillin), and being called to the Torah in the synagogue.

I had already experienced my brother's bar mitzvah, and was happy to have such a big celebration held now in my honor. This was a festive occasion, on which we all went together to the synagogue and later held a large feast at home. I was naturally very anxious during my *Drasha,* the bar mitzvah address, but everything went well and I also enjoyed the many gifts I received. All my school friends came the following day for a visit. My cousin Bella announced, "I will give you a gift that you and your friends will never forget."

I had no notion of what she had up her sleeve, and was very curious to know what her plans were. I have no idea how she managed it, but she brought an ice cream vendor, complete with horse and cart, to my bar mitzvah celebration. Today this would be no big deal, but in those days it was really extraordinary, and especially at a religious celebration. The adults were shocked by the appearance of a horse at such a religious gathering — but my friends and I were fascinated and delighted.

But the ice cream cart was not the only aspect of my bar mitzvah that caused excitement. Before the bar mitzvah, one is taught for a while by the rabbi, becomes familiar with the basic principles of the Jewish religion, and learns how to read the haftarah, a supplemental chapter from the Prophets, which is read after the Torah portion. Our rabbi was an exceptionally unpleasant teacher, and had the most painful habit of pinching us on the knee whenever we were wrong or did not know the answer to a question. I thought this so unjust I wanted to take revenge by playing a prank. I hid a piece of a broken plate under my pants, above the knee, and when he again tried to pinch me, he only hurt his fingers. He was furious and pulled my ear. Even though the ear pull was even more painful than the pinch, I got great satisfaction from my scheme.

In spite of my pranks I was called to the Torah in the synagogue in June of 1939, and the many gifts I received compensated for the unpleasant learning experience. My parents gave me a real watch, a Tissot, and I was immensely proud of it. It was a very expensive gift for those times, and not many received such things from parents for their bar mitzvah. The suit, the clothes, and my other new possessions pleased me very much, but they could not compete with the watch.

The watch made it simpler to keep arrangements to go to the movies, which I did often. Many films were screened in Kaunas, and the American Westerns especially appealed to me. One ticket was sufficient for two people for the afternoon show, but the theater was one of the places where we tried our luck at getting in for free. I was well known as a "crasher," but since I always thought of some nice conciliatory gesture in advance, no one could be angry with me for long. I had a very active, broad-based social life, and this helped me to make friends easily. It was a youth full of adventure and antics. Even the springtime floods caused by the great river, the Niemunas, which flowed through Kaunas, were for me not a catastrophe but an adventure. We lived pretty close to the river, and one night the water suddenly reached our door. It seeped into our living room, and we had to quickly move to a neighbor's apartment on the second floor. We stayed there for over a week, until the water receded and our apartment was again habitable.

For me, as a child, this was a fascinating experience — to sail between houses in a boat. Another time, when a flood again made our house uninhabitable, we moved to the house of relatives, who lived on a hill in Kaunas. This family had a daughter my age, in the same class as me. She was very pretty and particularly proud of her hairstyle. I suggested that if we played hairdresser she could be even more beautiful, as I would make her an especially lovely hairdo. After some hesitation she agreed, and I took the scissors and a comb and cut off her bangs. Unfortunately, the look was not exactly to her liking, and she cried all day. She stayed furious with me for a long time. She now lives in Tel Aviv, and to this day she reminds me that I still owe her a trip to the hairdresser!

First grade for me was disappointing. On my first day of school I came home weeping instead of happy, and complained: "I want to learn, not play." My brother and my cousin had already worked with me on the lessons for that first year, and when I entered the classroom that day, everything seemed like kindergarten to me. But the principal took pity on me and gave me a test that allowed me to move up to the second grade right away.

Looking back now, I understand that ours was a very good school, and I had exceptional luck with my teachers. They were not just instructors but really educators. One day our entire class went on a field trip, and on the way there we met a group of Gypsies. There were quite a few Gypsies in Lithuania at the time, and they were often treated badly, with very little respect. And so they also became the target of our mockery. Our teacher took us quietly aside and started a conversation about nature's many species, and about the differences between human beings, with regard to language, religion, and color of skin. He explained to us that the Gypsies' tradition was different from ours, but that no one should be discriminated against because of his culture, customs, or convictions. This conversation, in which he urged us to show tolerance toward others, became deeply engraved in my consciousness.

Given their Zionist outlook, my parents took it for granted that after four years in elementary school my brother and I would move to the Hebrew high school in Kaunas. With the exception of foreign-language lessons, the language of instruction there was Hebrew, which I often used when speaking with my brother. In general, the curriculum resembled that of the other schools, except that we were also taught Jewish history and the Bible. All this greatly reinforced the sense of Jewish identity at our school. The pupils there also played a lot of sports, and regular matches were held with other schools. Sports was not a major interest of mine, but despite my small stature, I was a good basketball player, and I often interfered in the games of the bigger boys. As a result, a good friend of mine, who was a year older than my brother (and currently lives in Switzerland), often used to just grab me and beat me up. Today we frequently joke about the number of blows that I still owe him.

We had very easygoing relations with girls in those days and were often involved in coed sports activities. One of my classmates, Judith, who was also my neighbor, was a real tomboy. She was very athletic, and sometimes we had a contest, just for fun, to see who would dare to pinch her from behind as she flexed her muscles. Another of my classmates at the time was a girl who had escaped from Germany with her family. Ina's passion was ballet; she even danced sometimes in the State Ballet. For us, her fellow students and friends, it was always a great occasion when we were allowed to attend a performance. I can still recall how Ina, the prima ballerina, stayed loyally by my side during a long bout of diphtheria and tried to boost my spirits. I had to stay in bed for a month and was allowed no visitors. It was wintertime. Winters in Lithuania are very cold, and temperatures of minus 20 degrees are nothing unusual. In order to keep the room I stayed in warm, we used to put cotton-wool between the windowpanes of the double-glazed windows, and use a salt-filled container to absorb the moisture. Despite the freezing cold, Ina came by daily. She stood on tiptoe outside my window and carried on a sign-language conversation with me. Whenever my brother saw her coming, he'd say, "Your beloved is coming," which naturally embarrassed me, but amused the rest of the family. I always had some girlfriends with whom I passed the time.

At the age of ten, like many students from my class, I joined the General Zionist youth movement. Many of our activities were similar to those of the Boy Scouts — for example, camping in tents in the forest. Among ourselves we spoke Hebrew and sang Hebrew songs. We often discussed the possibility of a trip to Palestine: the preparations required for such a trip, the best time to go, and what we would do there. We sometimes attended lectures at school that were given by people who had just been to Palestine and who spoke about their experiences. Life on a kibbutz was a focus of many discussions, as the liberal General Zionists also had a small kibbutz movement.

We avoided controversy with other Zionist groups, including Betar and Shomer Hatsair, to avoid drawing unnecessary attention to ourselves or creating too much public exposure. But we held many debates with them. The various groups all agreed, however, that the important things to maintain were our Zionist conviction and Jewish identity, which wasn't easy in those times. Therefore, we held regular study sessions, designed to bring youngsters closer to Zionist ideas. This "Zionist basic education" often took place in the form of a camp with tents and was very popular among Jewish youngsters.

The writings of Leo Pinsker, a doctor from Odessa and one of the first Jews to assimilate, had a lasting influence on me. When pogroms broke out in Russia in 1881, Pinsker started to view the establishment of a homeland in Palestine as the answer to the officially sanctioned anti-Semitism around him. In 1882, he wrote his famous work, *Auto-Emancipation*, motivated by the czars' revocation of the emancipation promise. In the book, Pinsker wrote about the psychological and social causes of anti-Semitism, and warned that the existence of the Jews as an ethnic group within other nations was a situation that had to be quickly remedied. One of Pinsker's theses was to my mind particularly convincing at the time: He argued that Jews in all countries had, practically speaking, no future, since they could never fully assimilate. What they needed was a Jewish state — other nations would recognize them as equals only when they stood on equal footing with them in political and economic terms. He compared Judaism without a state of its own to a foreign body inside an organism. Pinsker was also of the opinion that the Jews had to stop identifying themselves as "special," a "chosen people" with no home. For to be viewed this way was to remain foreign in every country.

We also read and discussed the works of A. D. Gordon, a Tolstoy-inspired socialist who advocated the return of the Jews to the land, to the cultivation of property. In his theses one can already discern the concept of "the religion of work." Gordon not only presented his world outlook on paper but also fulfilled it in his own life. At the age of forty-eight he immigrated to Palestine and labored in orange groves. For him, working the land and cultivating the soil was equal to prayer and was at the same time a "legal" way of purchasing the property. If you work the land, it belongs to you. For him, manual labor was also an important element in generating a "national feeling" among the Jews in Palestine. The radical realization of his ideas in his own life made him a most important model for the pioneer movement in Palestine. A folk song from the pioneer period reflects the spirit of these times with the words "We came to Israel, to build here and to be built" (*Anu Banu Artza, Livnot U'lehibanot Ba*).

This longing for Israel was reflected not only in the songs of the Jews in Palestine but also in our verses and our hearts in Lithuania. The demand for a state, for a Jewish home, was the main motivation behind our Zionist work. This passion was by no means lessened by the invasion of the Russian army that took place at this time; on the contrary, it made me all the more determined. During this period, we had been hearing of the terror of Hitler, and realized the danger he presented. But no one dreamed he would overrun Russia. We actually felt safe from him.

3

CLOUDS OF OPPRESSION

In 1940, Lithuania — and therefore Kaunas as well — was occupied by the Russian army. I still remember clearly the day the Russians invaded. We were sitting in the garden when we first heard the tanks rolling down the street. Already that same day our Zionist organizations had been banned. Zionism was now deemed a crime, and the occupying forces tried to totally paralyze Zionist life.

I was fourteen years old when I learned what it meant to live under occupation. It was a somewhat grotesque situation. Many of our neighbors thought the Russian invasion to be the lesser of two evils, compared to a possible German occupation. My parents also reacted ambivalently to the events. On the one hand, they said, "better the Soviets than the Germans"; better communism than national socialism; better "to remain alone" than to be annexed like Poland and other countries. One consoled oneself with the thought that Russia was a power that could overwhelm the Germans in case of emergency.

On the other hand, immediately after the invasion, the confiscation of property began, and with it the persecution of the Lithuanian bourgeoisie, to which many Jews belonged. The situation worsened significantly, and the fact that Lithuania had lost her sovereignty became increasingly apparent. This was reflected in daily life, as the Lithuanian Communists took over the government and arrested many "enemies of the state." Other prisoners were arbitrarily released. The former bourgeoisie was the target of the unbridled hatred of the lower classes, who let their resentment run wild. Wealthy Lithuanians and Jews, therefore, suffered under the new government. Members of the bourgeoisie were sent to Siberia, and no distinction was made between Jews and Lithuanians. Of course, officially, the Lithuanians had their own state and their own president, but in actual fact they were subject to Russian rule, and the Russian military controlled the streets. The Lithuanians looked with great disfavor on the Jewish population since Jewish Communists were involved in the new regime. Later on, when the Germans invaded, they, along with others, bitterly took their revenge. The claim was that all Jews were Communists and had betrayed Lithuania.

Thanks to my father's profession, our family did not have to suffer very much from the confiscations. As an employee of a construction company that carried out many public projects, my father still had, as before, an occupation and an income. We had fewer difficulties than those who were self-employed. Still, the occupation had tremendous repercussions on our school studies. Study hours were cut, and teaching was no longer conducted in Hebrew (which was banned), but in Russian and Yiddish. Even the teachers changed their political orientation. I personally experienced an example of what this change meant.

The Russians turned our former Hebrew school into a Yiddish school. I noticed that my history teacher did not seem very unhappy at this change of events. One day I said something and he became angry. He shouted at me in front of the entire class and scolded me with these words: "Birger,* you should become a true Soviet citizen!" I shouted back: "Nicht dein Masel!"—meaning, "Not on your life." My answer caused a great furor over the next few days, and was the talk of the entire school. But I was not ashamed of my Zionist, anti-Soviet outlook. We held a very clear line, even when many young people crossed over to the Soviet Young Pioneers camp.

Despite the tense situation, we tried not to lose our sense of humor and now and then we made fun of our occupiers. It was indeed funny when the wives of the Russian officers bought silk night-gowns in the shops and wore them to the opera, thinking this was the new fashion in evening dresses. One joke in particular was popular in the Jewish community: A Russian officer is asked about all kinds of things, and he always responds with: "Yes,

---

* Birger — "citizen" in Yiddish.

we have everything in Russia."

"Do you have . . . ?"

"Yes, we have everything."

"Do you have many factories?"

"Yes, we have hundreds of factories."

"Do you also have *tsures* [Yiddish for trouble, mishap]?"

To which the Russian officer promptly answers: "Yes, we actually have three factories that manufacture it!"

Unfortunately, we had little to laugh about in our Zionist groups, since they had been officially banned. After the Soviet invasion in 1940, we established a new underground Zionist movement, called ABC. (The three letters stood for Irgun Brith Zion, which means Zion Alliance Organization.)

ABC was a nonpolitical youth movement — nonpolitical in the sense that we had decided to rise above all political disputes and concentrate on our main objective, consolidating our identity as Zionists, which was clearly being threatened. We wanted to strengthen our identity and find a way to flee Palestine. The organization included young people between the ages of fifteen and twenty-one. It was set up in a quiet, conspiratorial way that proved to be extremely effective. We worked in small groups of three or four persons, and each person knew only the members of his or her respective small group. Because I was one of the founders, I was in a position to know more people and groups. There was a central committee, as well as liaisons between the various groups and between the committee and the small group leaders. This way, if one person got caught, he could tell very little and name very few names. I myself was active at the middle level of the movement and was a liaison person. As a result I knew some of the members of the central committee and, naturally, the person who was responsible for me. He was only two years my senior.

Our ABC had evolved out of various branches of the Zionist youth movement, and also continued to exist later in the ghetto. Our joint efforts were directed against the Soviet policy of banning our organization. We wrote, by hand, our own newspaper, a flyer entitled *Nitzotz* (Spark). The inspiration behind the name came from a poem written by the most important Zionist poet, Haim Nachman Bialik (1873–1934). The spark of a fire, a flame, which appears in several of Bialik's poems, symbolized for him the true ideal to which one devotes oneself heart and soul, and which represents society's or culture's highest values. For us, this spark stood for the ideals of man we wanted to convey in our Zionist work. Though Bialik wrote his poetry in Hebrew, and this is important in its interpretation, I wish to quote here some lines taken from the translation of the poem "Nitzotz" to convey the basic thought of the poem and of our ideal:

MY SPARK

*One spark is hid in the fortress of
my heart,*

> So small, but mine alone;
> I asked it of no man, I stole it not,
> 'Tis me, and my own.
> And when my heart is broken
>   'neath the hammer
> Of torments and their curse,
> This spark wings out, flies up into
>   my eyes,
> And thence into my verse.

Our organization was anything but a harmless meeting of young people. We were no longer children and no longer had time for games. The political situation had pushed us too early into the role of adults. It was clear to us that the future existence of the Jewish people was in danger, and every effort had to be made to preserve Jewish identity. We had to find ways that, in spite of the Russian occupation, would lead us to Israel and allow us to realize our Zionist dream there.

Our efforts were mainly of a cultural nature. Shortly after the Russian invasion and the prohibition of Zionist groups and the banning of Hebrew, we decided to save as many Hebrew books as possible from our school library. So one night we broke into the school and made numerous trips carrying out several hundred books to be hidden in my family's garden house. It was indeed a truly daring act, and who knows what would have happened to us if we had been discovered by someone. But, fortunately, everything went smoothly and the books were safely hidden away.

Naturally, the absence of the books was noticed the next day, and a great commotion ensued. The theft was reported to the authorities and inquiries began immediately. Since I had long been known to be a Zionist activist, my name was immediately linked with the break-in. I was summoned by the police and interrogated for hours. But I consistently denied having any knowledge of the break-in or having had anything to do with the missing books. Even when it was threatened that my family would be sent to Siberia — which in those times was always on the agenda — I continued to bluff and play innocent. I was held by the KGB for twenty-four hours and underwent quite a brutal interrogation. Those twenty-four hours seemed to me like twenty-four years. I was only fourteen at the time, and I don't know where I found the strength to go through this ordeal and face the threat that my family would be banished. Among other things, it had to do with my conviction about our Zionist goals and the rightness of our actions.

When I was finally released, I ran home to see if my family was still there. I had no idea whether the interrogators had executed their threat or not. I can hardly describe my relief when I found them at home. To this day I believe nothing happened to them because of the prestigious position my father held at the time. Of course I had told my parents nothing about our actions, and they were terribly worried, since they had received no news about my whereabouts. But despite their anxiety, they said nothing about it at all, and I am certain they secretly supported me. They never told me *not* to go to the ABC, but simply refrained from asking where I went.

The garden hiding place became too risky after a while, and we distributed the books among various members of the group. Many managed to read the books, circulated in secret fashion, and were able in this way to at least reinforce their Jewish identity by practicing Hebrew. In all of our activities, we devoted time to plotting and planning how we might travel through Romania, Russia, and the other countries that lay between Kaunas and Palestine.

But soon our dreams would burst like soap bubbles. The German invasion of Lithuania and war with Russia marked the beginning of the bloodiest and cruelest war in history—and our still somewhat organized world was turned upside down.

4

THE GERMAN INVASION
TERROR AND DEATH

Shortly after the German assault on Russia was launched, Lithuania was occupied by the Wehrmacht. The German occupation quickly distinguished itself from that of the Russians. Lithuanian hoodlums now suddenly began to run wild, deciding to settle old accounts from the days of the Soviet occupation. This caused anti-Semitic riots on the part of Lithuanians, as Jews were arbitrarily robbed and shot. Newly formed gangs went from house to house, broke down the doors, ordered the Jewish tenants over to the wall and shot them, without batting an eye. It was no longer safe to walk the streets; one faced the constant risk of being killed.

On the day the German troops arrived — June 22, 1941 — all the Jewish families from our yard assembled in my parents' apartment. We sat near the radio and listened nervously to news of the invasion. There were also unsettling reports about the rioting Lithuanians — we could see through our windows Lithuanian youths shooting randomly with their rifles. Though the news prepared us, in a sense, for the invasion—if one can really speak about being prepared in such a situation—we were completely taken aback by the Lithuanians' actions. We were afraid the vigilantes might come to our house, but, surprisingly, we were protected by the caretaker of our housing complex, Jonas, who closed the two iron gates to our yard, blocking the Lithuanian pack who stood there shouting uncontrollably in front of our yard. He told them that no Jewish families lived there, and after some hesitation the gangs moved on. A weight was lifted from our hearts, since we were not close to the caretaker. We were very surprised at his risking his neck in order to protect us. I later found out that he had been well compensated by all the Jewish families living in our complex.

When the Germans took over, they put an end to the massacring by the Lithuanians. A kind of order seemed to return. But who among us knew that after the small-scale, arbitrary murders by Lithuanians, a systematic extermination would now begin?

On July 12, 1941, the decree was issued to wear the yellow Star of David. A ghetto, where Jews would be confined, was set up in July and August in Slobodka, a suburb of Kaunas. The forced resettlement was announced everywhere: in the streets, on the radio, in the newspapers.

At one time, Slobodka was a center of Jewish culture in Lithuania. Many important yeshivas, or rabbinical seminaries, were located there, among them the famous Slobodka Yeshiva, a Talmud academy highly respected throughout Europe. The academy was sponsored by an ultraorthodox society and characterized by profound religiosity and piety.

But before the ghetto was established in this part of the city, the Lithuanians carried out a bloody massacre there, with the Germans' tacit approval. Synagogues were desecrated and plundered, Torah scrolls were burned publicly, and thousands of people, mostly rabbis and yeshiva students, were murdered. News of all of this, of course, also reached our ears, and no one dared to speculate out loud about the events to come. Would we also be victims of a massacre, or had other plans been made for us?

Our family resettled like the others. We had to move so quickly that we barely had time to discuss the events unfolding in the family. Everything we could take with us was immediately packed. It was the first time in my life I had to carry a load like a hard laborer. I felt like a heavily laden donkey and almost collapsed under the weight. Each family was allowed to take a few personal effects — clothing, jewelry, a few pieces of furniture — which we transported on a borrowed wheelbarrow. Also one or two books. That was all. We had to leave behind almost all our property, which remained in place — we could not even sell it.

Our entire family was allotted one small room in the ghetto. We were only four at the time, because my cousin was already on her way to Moscow to join her husband. A small family in an even smaller room.

A short time before the ghetto was cut off from the outside world, the authorities announced that they needed five hundred university students and academic graduates to report for work in the municipal archives. Students and young professionals happily packed their report cards and diplomas with hopes that their good education, to which many Jewish parents had pushed their children, would prove to be worthwhile. Confident that they would find an adequate position and be able to support their families, they went to the specified place and were immediately transported from there. No one ever saw or heard from them again. A few days later we learned they had all been shot dead by machine-gun fire on the outskirts of Kaunas.

Though we had lost everything — house, occupation, most of our belongings — we were nevertheless still alive and together. My father, brother, and I were assigned to different work groups, and so we went our separate ways every morning. I was sent to one of the small workshops set up in the ghetto to manufacture equipment and make repairs for the German army.

In the beginning I was arbitrarily assigned work as a plumber, but I could just as easily have been given the position of electrician or cook. Since I showed some skill in this area, I was later able to work in the locksmith's workshop and "advance my training." The workshops were set up in what had once been factory buildings, and there were a few genuine skilled workers who trained us and supervised our work. Those who were not entirely incapable of picking up the various skills were allowed to work independently. I quickly became an independent workman, not so much because of my talent, but because I made a concerted effort to be regarded as a valuable worker: My work permit was a matter not of prestige but of survival.

As a craftsman I even had a bit of freedom, which I took advantage of to fashion a tin box for myself. I decorated it with imaginative designs and was very proud of my small work of art. I then took the few remaining treasures we had at home and put them in the box: all of our family's important documents, photographs of my brother and me helping to harvest hay during vacation, a picture of my grandparents and parents, school photographs of my friends, and also a small diary. I packed all this into my box and buried it in our yard one night.

The task of assigning jobs was taken on by a Jewish committee, which the Germans called the Judenrat (Jewish Council). The chairman of this committee was Elchanan Elkes, a man who contributed very much to the respect and recognition the committee enjoyed. The election of the Council of Elders, in which the thirty community leaders of Kaunas had the right to vote, had been a very dramatic event. Electing a chairman seemed especially difficult, since this was a person who had to combine as many positive qualities as possible: He had to be popular in the community, enjoy great respect, and be a "good" Jew — one who is humane, clever, courageous, and of strong character. But he also had to be sure of himself when appearing before the Germans. After much discussion, it was finally decided that Dr. Elkes was the best candidate.

At first he turned down the position, but it was made clear to him that he had a moral obligation to accept the task, and could not shirk this responsibility. He finally agreed. In retrospect, this choice turned out to be a wise decision on the part of the Jewish community. Dr. Elkes was very conscientious, and never made it easy on himself when he had to draw up lists for the Germans of those to be sent to labor camps. Indeed, no one in the ghetto would have wanted to be in his position. The committee members were respected members of the Jewish community, committed to Zionism, and disputes with ghetto residents were rare, as everyone knew that the tasks were not easy and were carried out with the utmost deliberation.

My mother was not assigned to any work groups, and was able to stay at home. That did not mean that her life was in any way tranquil, but at least she was able to make sure that our small room was kept tidy, that we had clean clothes and something to eat and did not get lice.

After a while, my work at the locksmith's workshop proved to be an unexpected blessing for our family — it made it possible for me to save a diamond that we had hidden away.

In September 1941, the Germans let it be known

that all valuables in the ghetto would have to be handed over. They were to be placed on the kitchen table, and squads of soldiers would march from one flat to the next and confiscate the valuables. If anyone was caught holding precious stones or gold after one of these so-called *Aktionen*— which were usually announced beforehand over loudspeakers — he would suffer the severest consequences: He himself would be shot, along with his family and an additional one hundred Jews. Since my father and I had been expecting an *Aktion* for a long time, we had removed the metal fittings of the lock and door handle of the door to the flat in order to drill a hole underneath. In this hole we hid my mother's large diamond. But very early one morning, an SS Kommando came to our house with a group of Lithuanians and ordered us to immediately clear the apartment. The entire barrack, around fifteen rooms, was to be evacuated without delay, for it was now needed as a headquarters. It all happened very quickly, and we barely had time to gather together our few valuable belongings.

We were fortunate in being able to move in with relatives, where we had to live with three families in the most circumscribed space. The move happened so suddenly, it was impossible for us to take the diamond with us, and so it was left in its hiding place in the door. Luckily, it was not found when the SS searched the rooms shortly thereafter.

Our room became the ghetto commandant's

office, a man who had no scruples about sending
people to their death and who generated an atmosphere of terror, the like of which I have never experienced since. The idea of ever getting back the
diamond was totally abandoned, and we had to
come to terms with the fact that we'd lost this last
bit of financial security. But this is where my locksmith's job came in handy.

One day a soldier came to the workshop with an
order that a locksmith immediately be sent to the
headquarters. Given the fact that one was likely to
encounter the dreaded commandant on this occasion, it wasn't surprising that no one wanted to go.
Without the slightest hesitation, however, I called
out, "I'll go!" Everybody looked at me in shock.
My workmates thought I had lost my mind. I tried
to appear calm and collected as I packed my toolbox and started off for the headquarters. Three
doors down from the commandant's room, one of
the locks was broken, and I was able to repair it
easily. This was my big chance. With a little luck,
I would be able to take our diamond, and with a lot
of luck, no one would notice. I don't believe I even
gave it much thought—I had only one thing in my
head: that this rock could provide our family with
food for some time. If I had started to contemplate
the danger in this situation, I would surely have left
the diamond in its place.

So I pretended that I also wanted to check the
other locks and slowly worked my way over to
the commandant's office where our diamond was

hidden. I checked the door next to the commandant's office, then the commander's door itself. Suddenly an SS man called out:

"Hey, what are you doing?"

"I am checking the locks!"

"All right, but be quick, before the Obersturmbannfuehrer comes!"

Trembling, I removed the lock, extracted the diamond, and, unnoticed, dropped it into my toolbox. I quickly replaced the lock and made off. Only in retrospect did I realize what a risk I had taken. We were later able to exchange bread and potatoes for the diamond — in the ghetto, such edibles were more valuable than all the precious stones in the world.

Hunger gnawed deeper with each passing day, the rations only diminishing. It became increasingly important to get hold of additional food if we wanted to survive. We took no meals in the small workshops inside the ghetto. It was different in the work details on the outside. There we were provided with a meal that we called *Juschnik*: a soup made with a couple of potatoes or potato peels; actually there was nothing to it. But sometimes a work group was able to find a piece of meat in it — this was what one aimed for. Shared family meals became a thing of the past. We sometimes sat together around the table in the evening and talked about how we would make it through the coming days. There was nothing much to eat unless we had managed to exchange something and get hold of a few potatoes or bread, but that was the exception rather than the rule.

In order to obtain such delicacies, for example, I pawned the watch I had received from my parents for my bar mitzvah. My brother went outside the ghetto walls and purchased a sack of potatoes for it. I was then able to smuggle the sack into the ghetto, and we divided the "booty" amongst the family. Eventually everything was divided, and no one thought of keeping anything extra for himself. In this way we sold all our belongings — first my watch, then the diamond, and finally my mother's golden wedding necklace. It was a very long necklace, and we sold it one link at a time. Out of the earnings we were able to buy bread and potatoes and survive the most difficult of times.

Conversations in the family and with friends always revolved around one subject: food. At the beginning we were still quite resourceful and baked cakes or made "liver" from lentils. This was called liver only because we spiced the lentils in the same way one spices liver, and afterwards fried it. We yearned for some variety in the dishes, and so my mother created the illusion that we still had a choice, even if most of the time potatoes or bread were what was being served. She dreamt up many new recipes in this way — the wealth of ideas she came up with was amazing. One day my mother announced: "Food is ready. Today we're having cake!" We wondered how there could suddenly be a cake, when for months we hadn't even the ingredients needed to make one. We sat down at the table in rapt anticipation and were rather astonished when our mother finally served us a cake she had baked using carrots. It was excellent, almost as good as a real cake. But the worse the food situation got and the greater our hunger, the harder it became to talk about food.

Still, even though the food shortage hung over us daily like the sword of Damocles, in retrospect those days did not seem nearly as oppressive as the later period spent in the camp. In the ghetto one was hungry, but in the camp people really did starve.

In spite of the tense situation and the daily struggle against despair, I cannot recall any quarrel or friction in our family. On the contrary, I had the impression that the cramped situation and shared worries brought us even closer together. I never knew of any loud difference of opinions between my parents. If there were any, my brother and I never heard them. The patterns of human relations we grew up with would play a large role in our lives; in this sense, we were well-educated by our parents. This was most noticeable when we had to live together in a very confined area and there was next to no private space anymore.

After moving in with our relatives, we lived in an apartment together with three other families. Some distant relatives of ours—my second cousin and her daughter (the victim of my haircut), whom I have referred to as my cousin since that time, slept in one room. My sleeping area was in a corridor-like corner, and a young couple arranged a place behind a curtain. Their furniture consisted of a small bed, nothing else. My parents lived in another room and my brother also slept there. A couple of siblings with their respective spouses also lived in the same apartment, but they frequently quarreled among themselves, and the atmosphere was often tense. A poorly equipped kitchen and one lavatory in the corridor were used by all of us. Despite the lack of privacy, things went on in a friendly manner.

In fact, I have to admit that at times the cramped quarters produced a pleasant side-effect. It was so overcrowded in the apartment, one could barely move without brushing someone's shoulder or another part of the body. So when I walked across our room, I was often forced to touch my "cousin," who was my age. And this was by no means an unpleasant feeling. I refer to her as a cousin, because all relatives who were not siblings or parents I labeled cousin, uncle, or aunt. All the relatives my age were cousins, the grown-ups were uncles and aunts. I have kept this habit up until today, even if it sometimes confuses others when I talk about assorted relatives and refer to them as cousins although they are actually very distant relatives.

The friendly atmosphere that characterized daily life in our "collective flat" was by no means the rule everywhere, and there were many ugly scenes among the ghetto inhabitants. It was increasingly difficult for people to bear the uncertainty, shortage of space, and isolation from the outside world. People quarreled over trivial matters. I found this difficult to understand, since we behaved differently with one another. We had good relations also with our neighbors, and we helped each other.

At irregular intervals the Germans carried out their Aktionen. On these occasions the ghetto was sealed off, and no one was allowed in or out. We could not go to work on these days, but were forced to assemble in the square, and on the bare, hard-packed soil we were lined up in rows. The SS officers passed among the rows, heads held high, lashing their whips. They struck out at the assembled people according to their whim, or beat them for no reason. People were sent to the right or the left, with everyone aware that to the right meant work and to the left meant death. What we did not know was if they were sent directly to be killed, or to Estonia, or to a work camp. We would stand for hours in that square, watching helplessly as families were torn apart, young people separated, and grandparents taken away from their children and grandchildren. I can still see the impassive faces of the German soldiers who carried out this task without any emotion whatsoever.

Our work permit also protected us at first from being deported. The labor done in the ghetto workshops was important for the German military, and we harbored the false hope that as long as we did good work, we would not be transported.

But it was not only the official "selections" of

those unfit for work that disrupted the regular course of the day; above all, it was the arbitrary shootings from which we could find no rest. In the first half of the year following the establishment of the ghetto, murder was a daily occurrence; you could never know when it would strike you or a family member. Soldiers simply pulled ghetto residents off the street or dragged them out of their houses and, for no reason, stood them against the wall and shot them, or brought them to the Ninth Fort, part of an old fortification, to be shot.

One day when one of the ghetto Aktionen was getting under way, I was with a friend near the barn in our courtyard when we heard the soldiers coming. We quickly went inside the barn and hid on the floor of the hayloft above. Just as we disappeared into the hay, the door was pushed open and the soldiers burst in with their bayonets raised. They searched the room, but did not climb up. Just as we started to breathe freely again, they pushed their bayonets from below between the wooden boards of the hayloft above. We barely dared to breathe, and when the tip of a bayonet point was thrust through the hay and appeared between my friend and myself, I thought the clock had struck my last hour. Drenched in sweat, we stared at each other. And, indeed, each one was thinking the same thing. But the next stab again missed us, and after a futile search and a few minutes that seemed like an eternity, the men left the barn.

To lower our morale to zero and obliterate all

hope for the future, the so-called Children Aktion was carried out in the Kaunas Ghetto on March 27, 1944. While we, like everyone else who was fit for work, were doing our jobs in the workshops, and only the old people and mothers were at home with the small children, an order was issued to bring all children up to a certain age to a particular place.

Not everyone obeyed the order. Many had prepared hiding places long before, in which they now tried to hide their children. False floors in closets, camouflage in front of walls, and small hideaways in cubicles were designed to keep the little ones from being seized by the Germans. But the soldiers searched the ghetto house by house, and not a single child managed to escape. Mothers who wanted to accompany their children were pushed back, and those who attempted at least to save their own lives were forced to accompany the children.

This Aktion lasted two days, and the night between was characterized by desperate thoughts as to what one could do in order to save the children. But it was all in vain. My future father-in-law, whom I never met, risked his life during these two days, trying to hide a group of about a hundred children who were a bit older in the attic of the Council of Elders building. He thought the Germans would not go through this house. But he was wrong, and had to pay for this with his life. He was taken together with the children to the Ninth Fort and shot.

With the children gone, a ghostly quiet descended on the ghetto streets and courtyards. No more laughing, no more games, no more running wild — only emptiness remained. In the course of the Children Aktion, more than two thousand children were murdered, and with them the hope of a new beginning.

A very small number of mothers had managed to save their offspring, by wrapping the babies in warm sheets and throwing them over the fence at night to be taken into the care of Lithuanian farmers who were paid large sums of money. But this was also very unsafe, and no one could know what happened to the children. Yet one was at least able to retain some glimmer of hope, and did not have to hand over the children directly to their executioners. Some children were saved this way, but no one knew how many of them had the good fortune to be taken in by decent people.

After the Children Aktion, we became more conscious of the importance of our Zionist work with the youth in the ghetto. All our expectations were now transferred to them. Now that the smallest children were no longer there, the youth became the hope of the Jewish residents — we simply had to save them.

We continued the organization in conspiratorial ways and even expanded it. In coordinating with other groups of the underground movement, we established three objectives: further cooperation with the partisans (guerrilla groups fighting against the Nazi occupation) outside the camp; the construction of underground bunkers inside the ghetto, in which people could hide for many days in case of emergency; and, finally, the struggle against submission, the insidious demoralization and dehumanization behind the barbed wire. We had to give to these young people a sense of confidence, a meaningful occupation, and the expectation of a future in which one could live with equal rights, so that they would not lose courage.

A good opportunity for this was the organization of a kind of "Jewish police" to guard several fields. There were a couple of uncultivated fields, which the Ghetto Committee was allowed to use for growing potatoes to distribute to ghetto residents. In order to prevent the potatoes from being stolen before thcy were ready, we set up a guard watch with the youngsters who had yet to join the work detail, and they guarded the fields around the clock. This gave the members a meaningful occupation, and they had the feeling that they were contributing in an important way to the survival of the community. We even wore a kind of a uniform of white sailor caps, which marked us as "policemen." The youth were thirteen to sixteen years old, and naturally very proud of their white caps.

At the same time the youth police acted as a cover for our underground Zionist work. I was entrusted by the ABC leadership with the establishment and organization of the group protecting the potato and vegetable fields, which was under the supervision of the Elders Committee. Being in charge of this task, I lived with the constant fear that the Germans would come and eliminate our whole organization and take us to the Ninth Fort to be shot. One could never be certain one day whether we'd still be able to function the next.

But up until the evacuation of the ghetto this did not occur, and we were able to continue our work. We gave the youngsters whatever Hebrew books were still available, spoke Hebrew with them, and taught them self-defense techniques — after all, they did have to look after the fields. The camouflage proved its worth in the long run, and no one noticed our ideological studies. This was an emergency collective, a union of young people who did not know whether they would survive the night but did everything in order to be well-equipped for a new life at the end of the war.

For many who had lost their relatives, we were the replacement for family and friends. They found in us something to cling to. Some were only a few months in the organization before they would disappear. It was a terribly ambivalent feeling: to build up the greatest possible bond between individual members, but always with the knowledge that anyone could be torn from us at any time.

For our work it was important that there be next to no conflicts between the individual subgroups, the Jewish Committee, and the underground movement. We worked well with the ghetto police, which was no doubt to a great extent due to our commander, Ika Greenberg. Unlike in other ghettos where the idea and execution of an armed resistance resulted in many disagreements with the elders, this was a question that never even arose with us. It was impossible for us to organize something like an armed resistance. Where would we get arms from in the hostile environment of the Lithuanians? Naturally, we debated whether the underground endangered the entire ghetto, but the subject did not cause any open dispute. We used our energy for thinking, not for quarreling.

Our work was carried out without the knowledge of most ghetto residents; only a few in whom we had confided knew of our actions. The business of the united youth organization was educational — the Zionist-national education of the members and resistance work. Even in the worst times, when morale was at its lowest, such as after the Children Aktion, we attempted to discuss Zionism and literature. We often fantasized about what we would do when the war was over: where would we go, what would we do with our lives, how would we raise our children. We could by no means allow ourselves to lose courage or hope, because without hope one was as good as dead.

Our nocturnal activities included the construction of the underground bunkers, which were called *Malines*. We dug hiding places underneath the houses, redistributing the soil so that nothing could be noticed the following day, and were utterly exhausted in the morning when we had to go to work. The

Malines were proper cellars under the houses, around 1.8 meters high so one could stand quite comfortably in them, with concealed entrances. We hoarded food and water in them so that people could survive there for some time. By blocking old entrances and constructing new, hidden ones, we even transformed existing cellars into secret bunkers. Many ghetto residents probably sensed what was going on, but no one knew anything for certain.

I was almost never home at night. My parents immediately understood that meant that I was involved in the construction of the Malines. But they were against my hiding there if an emergency arose. What they wanted was for me to escape from the ghetto, because they knew that I had the contacts and connections to get by. They wanted at least one of our family to survive. Since I spoke Lithuanian with almost no accent, I had, at the beginning of the ghetto period, removed the yellow star now and again and left the ghetto. I obtained food for our family and established contacts with some Christians. One could not claim that I looked typically Lithuanian, but I wore a common cap to disguise myself so that no one would notice that I came from the ghetto. In this way I had the opportunity to observe the reaction of the Lithuanians when they saw the columns of Jewish workers moving through the streets to the detachments. How could they simply ignore what was so obvious? On these occasions I could feel just how much they hated the Jews. I was shocked not only by their conduct after the invasion of the Germans, but also by the fact that the Lithuanian and Ukrainian units did the dirty work for the SS. I never wanted to have anything to do with these people again. I was so deeply and lastingly shocked by the inhumane, almost animalistic conduct of the Lithuanians that a short time after the war I discovered I was no longer fluent in Lithuanian. Suddenly I could no longer utter sentences in this language that I had spoken as well as my mother tongue. Worried that there was something very wrong with my brain, I went to a doctor who determined that I had suffered such a shock from my observations outside the ghetto that a mental block now paralyzed my memory, preventing me from recalling this language. I have never since tried to master Lithuanian again.

Despite my family's pressure to join the partisans and flee, I remained with my loved ones. I could not and did not want to abandon my parents, but wanted to go to the bunker with them when the time came to evacuate the ghetto. So I made sure there was sufficient food and water in the Maline that was planned for us. My brother had already established contacts with the partisans, but he did not turn his intentions into action and so also remained with us. Unfortunately, as I must now say. With the partisans he might have had a chance of surviving.

My neighbors, of course, knew nothing about

my activities or what function I served in the organization. Even my parents had only the vaguest idea about our work, but knew there were things about which it was better not to ask questions. The issue of the partisans preoccupied us for quite a while. Who should and could join them? The most difficult questions within the organization were: Who should we send at all? Who should we send first? Who should we send later? Everyone in the underground movement agreed that the first ones to be sent should be those who no longer had any family in the ghetto. The leaders decided who went first, who went second, who third. The criteria used were truly significant. It was above all the single young people, whose families had been deported or murdered in an Aktion, who went. This was the case with three friends of mine, who had been in my class at school. Without parents and relatives they were left on their own in the ghetto. Therefore they joined the partisans. None of the three survived the war.

The escape system organized by the underground movement consisted of contacts established with Christian families outside the ghetto who were willing to hide Jews for money. An entire network was built on this basis, which was supposed to secure the escape. Some succeeded in escaping, others were captured while fleeing, some joined the partisans with whom we had direct contact. Many ghetto residents approached the organization and asked whether we could help them. Indeed, we could establish contacts, but we could guarantee nothing. Nevertheless, one of my closest relatives, my cousin Jutia, did survive this way. She was fluent in Lithuanian, presented herself as a Lithuanian, wore long braids, and lived with simple farmers in the country.

The ABC became an aid and support organization, whose main task was to find ways to enable at least some of the ghetto residents to survive. Cooperation with the Jewish Council functioned well. They allowed our underground movement to operate with silent consent — officially we did not exist.

The various factions of the underground organization worked in an entirely different manner from one another, and also held different objectives. But in spite of these differences, there was strong cooperation among the groups. In retrospect, I think that the ABC was the most committed to the ideals of Zionism.

During the time in the ghetto I also got to know Jascha, who has remained my best friend to this very day. He is my age and his father was my pediatrician. We often met together to talk after work, when darkness had already fallen. We encouraged each other and spoke at length of our plans for the time following the liberation from the ghetto. He was later with me in the camp and was like a brother to me. Through our nighttime talks we pulled ourselves out of the sea of despair and saved one another. It was during this time that I noted how much a conversation with someone you trust can mean, and how it could protect you from despair and resignation. We spoke about everything: politics, books, where our lives were headed. We had some very philosophical discussions about the meaning of life and mostly about the future. We were both sure that we would get through the war, and maybe this helped us to keep believing and never to give up hope. Later, in the camp, we not only supported each other through conversations, but we literally saved each other's life.

My brother Mordechai had meanwhile met a very attractive girl named Rivka, who was the only remaining member of her entire family. The young couple married in a modest ceremony in the ghetto. There was no wedding party — they simply went to the rabbi and became husband and wife. Afterwards, as a married couple, they moved into their own room — actually a corner of a room — in our flat. But their marriage lasted only a couple of months before they were separated forever. As I later found out, neither of them survived the war.

I also had a growing interest in girls and had a girlfriend in the ghetto. My young love, who was part of our group, was one year younger than me. We were often together and talked for hours. But when the ghetto was evacuated, her father, a very angular man of German origin, decided that the family would not hide in the bunker, but rather go directly by transport to the work camp in Germany. He allowed no objections — and so they were all killed.

Another friend, for whom I also felt deep affection, had the good fortune to survive. She came with many others to the surprise party on the occasion of my seventieth birthday, and seeing each other again was very moving for both of us, since I had been the last one to see her in the ghetto. She was a pretty young girl and wanted to escape, to go and hide with Lithuanian farmers. The night she fled I took her to the ghetto fence, close to the riverbank. As a farewell gift I gave her a simple wooden cross that I had crafted in the workshop. I hung the tiny cross around her thin neck and said: "You must wear this to stay alive. With this you will be taken for a Christian."

She wore it the entire time and indeed it helped her to pass as a Christian. I had entirely forgotten this story, but as she recounted it, I could once again picture the young girl near the dark river bank and how I had tried to encourage her. At least she had remained alive.

We worked hard the night before the evacuation of the ghetto, which finally took place on July 8, 1944. Up to this point, many underground bunkers in which Jewish families could hide had been built. However, one first had to decide if one wanted to take the risk of hiding in the Maline. But we went into our cellar without hesitation. A whole group, including many of my friends from the underground movement, joined us in our bunker. We heard the people above being driven together and pushed to the assembly square. Later the houses were blown up and the systematic search for those hiding began. The soldiers thoroughly searched house after house for "surviving souls" and were often successful in their search. We were able to stay hidden in our Maline for around five days, but we knew the entire time what was happening around us.

I ventured to look outside for a second, to see what was happening. The ghetto had almost been wiped out by the SS, and I heard shots close by. It was only a matter of days or hours before they would find us. But we clung to the only hope we still had: that we would remain undiscovered until the Russian army came. The Soviet front was already within earshot. But the German search groups were getting nearer. Finally we were discovered and dragged out of our hiding place. They dug up another bunker close by, and I had the feeling that we had been betrayed. So, on July 13, 1944, forced together with the remaining Jews in the community, approximately three to four hundred people, we were pushed toward the square. The Lithuanians had already started plundering the abandoned ghetto and began to dig systematically in the ground and under floors, searching for valuables. In the process they must have also found my tin box with the pictures and documents.

We, the wretched remainder of the ghetto residents, had to line up and walk to the gate leading to the railway station. At the same time, the people were sorted to the right or the left, the old and sick people to the left and the rest to the right. It was then that my mother was separated from us. I tried to hold on to her as tightly as I could, but one of the guards beat me brutally, knocking out several of my teeth. I lost consciousness for a short while, and when I came to, I saw how she was taken to the left with a group of old women and men. That was the last time I saw her. She stood there and raised her hands, to bless us. My father and my brother had to support me as we walked through the ghetto gate.

Despite the great confusion, everything went very fast, and we were pushed onto the train platform. Husbands and wives were separated and sent to different railway cars. My father constantly asked my brother and me to take advantage of the chaos and run away. But having lost our mother we did not want to lose our father as well.

There were already several cattle cars standing in the train station, and the Jews from the ghetto were crammed together onto them. We were all that was left of the Jews from Kaunas, and we were driven away on the last transport, which left the ghetto in the direction of Germany.

5

The Camps

A Surreal Suffering

Throughout the journey to Germany, which lasted several days, I was haunted by the picture of my mother, standing there with her hands raised high, imploring, "You at least stay alive!" It is an image that has not left me to this day. In nightmares that leave me drenched in sweat, I see my mother standing near the small group of elderly men and women, and I cannot reach her.

There were several opportunities during the transport to jump off the train and run for the woods, but my brother and I wanted to remain with our father under all circumstances, although he repeatedly begged us to escape. During the train ride I found a brick, which I used as a pillow in the car. After a few days we arrived at the Stutthof Concentration Camp, near Danzig. In a pandemonium of pushing and shouting, we were driven out of the train and entered a huge hall, where everything was taken from us: clothes, shoes, our last belongings. The items had to be placed on piles, systematically arranged, and then we were sent totally naked to the delousing facility. We were then pushed out into the open and there, from vast piles, we had to take our striped prisoners' clothes and shoes. We were allowed to keep nothing, not even the smallest trifle. Even my asthma medication, which I always carried with me, was taken away. But I not only lost my medicine — the shock also made me lose my asthma. During that time, my brother joked, "You see, the change of air was good for your health!"

We were transported from Stutthof to an unknown destination. Rumor had it that we were on our way to a work camp. It turned out to be Dachau.

In contrast to our first transport, the journey this time was very long. It was also summertime and therefore terribly hot in the cattle cars. We had been packed so closely together it was nearly impossible to lie down. There were peep holes in the tops of cars, through which we could make out the various stations. Augsburg, Nürnberg — names that meant nothing to me then. In Nürnberg we heard the sirens; by this time the war was no longer going in Germany's favor.

The sirens announced another air raid, and immediately afterwards we could hear the bombs falling right near our railroad cars. Confused, we realized that the war was now being waged on German soil, but at the same time, we were locked in and could not protect ourselves or run for shelter during air-raid attacks. We could be hit by a shell and sent flying sky-high with no warning.

We had only one bucket in the car to serve as a

lavatory, and the smell became unbearable. We often stood for hours in some railway stations and had no idea of the journey's destination. We knew nothing about the extermination camps; many thought that we were going to Germany to work. We were convinced that it would be better in Germany than in Poland, because the prisoners who had been transported to our ghetto had come from Poland. They told us there were extermination camps there. We did not want to believe such a thing.

The transport arrived at Dachau after about a week. However, the train did not stop at the railway station in the city, but continued directly into the camp. We only stayed for two days in the main camp, but in that time we heard about the crematoria. The hope that we would be put to work proved to be false. We now knew what awaited us. Dachau was no longer just a name for us, it now became the symbol of our planned extermination. A few days later we were transported to one of Dachau's external camps, Camp IV, together with the other Jews from Kaunas and a few from other countries.

We arrived at Camp IV, Kaufering, and passed the sign that denoted our new lodgings: "K.L. Dachau, L.B. Kaufering, L.IV" — Dachau Concentration Camp, Kaufering Camp District, Camp IV. There we were put to work as slave laborers for the German armaments industry. Hiding behind the code name "Wood-Dove" was one of the last great armament projects of the Third Reich. The Nazi machine now found itself in dire straits in the wake of its defeats on all fronts, and was gearing up for one last push before the fall. Facing a desperate situation, they intensified their production of aircraft. The fighter planes so urgently needed for their air defense were to be produced in underground facilities as quickly as possible. Landsberg, along with Mühldorf am Inn, was chosen as one of the locations due to the high level of gravel found in the area. It was used for the construction of a relatively simple underground bunker. The gravel obtained from the excavation of the foundations was spread in an arched shape, and the bunker vault was constructed on top of this, out of many concrete-cast sections. Then the gravel was dug out and reused for the production of concrete. The dimensions of the construction were vast: The vault was huge—240 meters long, the inside width around 80 meters, and the inside height 25 meters. There were twenty-one locomotives and two hundred train cars in use at the work site. Naturally, I learned all of this much later.

When we entered the camp I could not see any barracks or other lodgings. Only long, low roofs rising from the ground like long tents. The roofs were covered with grass, and there were many rows of such field sheds. There was no electricity connected to the sheds, so we thought they were just air-raid shelters. But then we were divided into groups and led into the sheds. I was in the same group as my father and brother. Going down two steep steps we went through a narrow door into a long cellarlike room. It looked like a mine tunnel: With a sloping roof supported by beams, the area consisted of a lengthwise trench stamped into the ground, around 25 meters long. The only sources of light were the door on one side and the window on the other side of the shed. On both sides of the strips of ground, flat boards, nailed together, were fastened at knee height — on the surface of the ground — each serving as a bed for twenty-five people. Fifty people had to share this area, the roof of which consisted of boards arranged in sloped, tentlike fashion. Its highest point was above the lengthwise strips by the bed boards, where all the boards were fastened at an angle and attached to the ground. We slept with our heads in this corner. Later a brick chimney was built in the center above the roof, as a flue for the tiny stove that stood in the shed. The stove was the center of the shed, in more than just the physical sense.

After the exhausting journey most of us were so starved that only a few had the strength to work. Nevertheless, we were sent to work the next day. In the meantime we were given a new identity: We stood in a queue in the camp's orderly room in front of a writing stand. The camp clerk stamped a number on the personnel form, using an automatic numbering machine. This was my prisoner number, my new name: D 5046.

Early the next morning (it was actually still night), we marched by starlight to the railway tracks and on into the woods. After a bend we were suddenly blinded by a sea of lights. An enormous, mountain-high reinforced concrete arch was lit up, with countless iron bars protruding from it — it looked like an oversized hedgehog. Beside the dome was a huge pit, likewise filled with reinforced concrete. This infernal hole was called the death tank, and even the Kapos — Jews chosen to serve as foremen and heads of work details inside the camps — at Kautering said it was not easy to emerge from it alive. We walked another hour, passed a sea of rusted tow engines, dredgers, cranes, and other machinery that looked to me like sea monsters, until we finally arrived at the destination of our night walk: a huge reinforced concrete construction site. A giant dome was being built there, a hundred meters long, at least eighty meters wide, and around thirty meters high. It was a grotesque situation. I was impressed by the organization, ingenuity, and creativity of the German engineers — but at the same time appalled to think that these were the same minds that were responsible for mass murder. The Germans had invested all their intelligence, their technical ability, their work force for one objective: our death.

Inside the concrete hedgehog there was a construction site such as I had never seen in my life. Gigantic machines dug several ten-meter-deep pits, and in each cavity stood a network of iron rods. The entire structure was to be cast in concrete. The concrete was delivered by conveyor carts along the tracks, and the prisoners had to push the carts upward. The place was swarming like an anthill. Hundreds of tiny people — like the Lilliputians in *Gulliver's Travels*—were toiling away with urgency, and woe to them all if something wasn't finished on time.

First a huge gravel hill was piled up. This was covered with reinforced concrete. The noise was unbelievable: The machines and giant dredgers thundered underneath the sporadic sounds of orders being shouted, hammers slamming, whips thrashing, and prisoners wailing.

The work was very hard at the beginning when the concrete was still fluid, but it became thicker with time and held better; it was then possible to let a train run along the three meters of thick concrete that was supported from below. The gravel hill was several hundred meters long; it was supported on both sides by a reinforced concrete structure, sunk into the ground to a depth equal to this length, which contained the various passages and entrances, and all pipelines, cables, and wires. Thousands of people worked here, on the hill, in the pit, and on the countless frames and iron traverses.

We had to push the conveyor carts filled with concrete up the steep and hard but slippery concrete hill at a thirty-to-forty-degree angle. Powerful cement mixers had been positioned above, at the edge of the pit, and other machines transported the cement, gravel, and water needed at the spot. The mixers prepared the concrete that flowed steadily out of pipes, which were approximately 40 to 45 centimeters in diameter. We positioned the conveyor cart underneath one of the pipes, and when the cart was full of concrete, we moved it two hundred meters further and tipped it out. This way we leveled one layer after another. We worked on what was called the "Lower Edge." On the "Upper Edge"—the dome—the work was even worse.

At the summit, there were several construction sites where iron bars were being bent to the required length and shape. The iron bars were then transported by a train, driven by a locomotive. The locomotive made a terrible noise, and sometimes also got stuck. We then had to run quickly and shove large wedges under the wheels, to prevent the giant train from slipping backwards. Untold quantities of cement, train tracks, and cement mixers were transported to dizzying heights. The ground up above was very slippery; one had to hold fast to the rods to keep from slipping. Some no longer had the strength or will to hold on. They fell down from the concrete hill into the abyss, were mangled by the protruding iron bars, and landed in a bloody heap on the ground below. People were dying in great numbers from dragging the train tracks, or from the guards' whipping, or from falling down from the dome.

One morning, one of the SS men came accompanied by a civilian in a fur coat. He shouted, "Is there an electrician here?" Without thinking twice I answered, "Yes, I am an electrician." I could not imagine that work in another place could be any worse, which was why I had volunteered so quickly. The worst scenario was that the Germans would soon discover I was not an electrician, and would finish me off — but that was going to happen soon anyway, I figured.

An electrical engineer from AEG needed an assistant, and I was assigned to work with him. Naturally he noticed after just the first day that I had never studied this profession, but he said to me: "You are certainly no electrician, but you learn quickly. I still want to keep you on and see if you really can work." In this way he actually gave me a chance to live. This man still had human emotions and did not just obey orders. He had sympathy for me. My previous work in the ghetto, in the locksmith's workshop, had prepared me technically for this task. I worked well and was a great help to him. He was always very satisfied with my work and therefore treated me compassionately.

In the camp, there were many reasons for the sudden death of prisoners who had not died at work or been killed: Exhaustion and hunger, as well as the whipping and beating, took their daily toll. But there were also those who simply lost heart and the will to go on living. These people expired, just like candles that are blown out. In order to keep on going you had to tell yourself a hundred times a day: "I will survive. I will overcome this." I said this to myself as often as I could. On winter mornings I would wash myself with ice-cold water and hammer this sentence into my head.

I did not want to be snuffed out, I did not want to give up, I could not lose hope.

I was able to arm myself psychologically against hopelessness, but there was no protection from the terrible dysentery, which was taking its toll on more and more people in the camp. Anyone stricken with it could not retain or digest any food, and died within a few days from dehydration and exhaustion. Dysentery destroyed people in random fashion; they lost weight and became skeletons, their clothes just hanging from their bodies, and soon there was nothing left of them. Thousands and thousands in the camp died this horrible, wasting death, which usually did not even take three days. One morning I felt sick and discovered to my dismay that I, too, had the usual symptoms.

I went to my boss, the engineer, and said to him in a stammering voice, "You won't see me again and you will have to find a new assistant."

"Why?" he asked, puzzled.

I tried to explain the situation as best I could, but he said: "Nonsense! People don't die of the runs." He took a piece of his bread and put it on the stove to make toast for me, and though I couldn't actually eat or drink anything, I tried to get it down. He even gave me some to take with me to the camp. The next day, to my great surprise, he brought rice that had been prepared for me by his wife.

Thus, I slowly regained my strength and overcame this illness, which left most prisoners no chance for survival. I owe a great deal to the engineer and his wife, and I would have liked to thank them, but one morning when we reported for work, I was sent to another camp and had no opportunity to bid him farewell. I didn't even know his family name, and so I was unable to find him after the war. Thousands had worked with AEG at that time, and no one could help me in my search.

Life in the camp was a daily struggle for survival. You had to get food if you did not want to starve. I remember the day I was taken with a group of five or six people to pick up a machine part from the train station in Kaufering and load it onto a truck. We sat behind on the loading area and the driver sat in front with our guard. On the drive back from the train station we had engine trouble, and the truck had to stop. We were parked at the edge of a potato field. The guard and the driver got out on the other side of the vehicle, where they began fiddling with the engine. Without a second thought, I jumped off the truck, ran into the field, dug out several potatoes, hid them under my shirt and climbed back up to the loading area. It all happened so fast that most of the prisoners on the truck noticed nothing. When I returned, some thought I had been trying to escape and were so incensed they nearly beat me up. To them it was unfathomable that I had risked not only my life, but also theirs, and all for a couple of rotten potatoes. I tried to explain, to no avail, that I had to provide for my father. But they still thought I was out of my mind.

The pursuit of sustenance drove us into a dangerous conflict: On the one hand, we had to get food if we wanted to survive, but on the other hand, we could be shot on the spot if we were caught. What I had done might have been stupid, but it did help us to better endure the hunger for three or four days. On the evening of the same day we baked the potatoes on the stove in our shed, but since we were constantly afraid that someone would take them away from us, we ate them half raw.

Our situation could not be grasped in rational terms. What was our crime? We were being treated like animals, for having been born Jews. I felt trapped in a Kafkaesque reality, where there were no words to explain the charge against me. I moved around the camp like a hunted animal, and yet I had been caught long ago. The situation defied all reason.

A deep inner conviction, which I kept in sight every day and had to keep repeating to myself over and over, helped me not to lose my mind and expire like so many around me: I will survive! I will survive! I will overcome. I repeated these words over and over, day in and day out, in every situation I found myself. I did things that I never would have done under normal circumstances, such as washing with snow in order to toughen myself and remain healthy, with the sole purpose of staying alive. When it was freezing cold I convinced myself that it was warm, when it was hot, I tried to imagine it was cool. In this way I wanted to make each given situation livable, survivable. I lived as if in a dream, trying to blot out the reality of this surreal world. Wallowing up to our knees in mud I made myself believe that it was no big deal. It was a life-saving self-deception. I also used this "trick" every morning and evening in the assembly square, where scores of prisoners were collapsing from hunger and exhaustion. I said to myself: "Zev, you are not too tired nor too hungry to stand. Just another little while and then it will be over. Soon the end will come."

To encourage ourselves and to survive the walk from the assembly square to work, we sang marching songs, one of which was a Russian song that we sang in Yiddish: "To victory . . . for Stalin . . ." But of course we couldn't sing about Stalin, since our guards would have recognized the name even if they spoke no Russian or Yiddish. So we replaced the name with the Jewish expression for mustache—"wonse." Now every morning we struck up the tune and sang, "And when Wonse sends us, we'll go to work singing . . ." We also used the words "to work," instead of the original "to victory." During our daily march to work we were accompanied by guards from the Wehrmacht, elderly men to replace the young ones who had been taken to the front. One of these guards always used to say to us: "Sing the 'Wonse'"— he didn't know what it meant, but it was a good marching tune.

One winter morning the Kapo of our shed opened the door and began to shout. We could not understand a word, but after a quick glance outside we knew what had happened. Snow had fallen the night before, and the landscape was now wearing a pure white veil.

At home, in Kaunas, the first snow had always been a cause for joy. We used to play for hours in the white splendor, building snowmen and having snowball fights. I also remembered winter walks with my parents through the city park. How distant and unreal that life seemed. The snow now presented an additional threat for us. Snow meant freezing, death, increased suffering. Many thought of suicide when the snow got into their shoes or soaked their paper "shoes," the empty cement bags we wrapped around our feet and fastened with bits of wire. It was almost impossible to persevere with cold, wet feet, and this was our only protection.

The SS and our guards did not suffer from the cold. We knew because we had to provide the wood for their quarters. We plodded single file through the snow, with those in front stamping down a path for the others. After what seemed an eternity we finally arrived at a place in the forest where the woodpile stood. We were horrified to discover that the supply consisted of tree trunks and roots, weighing 25 to 30 kilograms, which we were supposed to heave on to each other's backs. We had several kilometers of snow to traverse ahead of us, and I had to convince myself yet again: "You will manage it. It's not impossible. The wood isn't actually pressing down on your back too much."

I felt I had no strength left, that I could not go on. The snow around me seemed like an endless desert, the icy wind blew in my face, and I could see nothing anymore. One of the prisoners fell down and no longer had the strength to stand up. The SS man shot him on the spot. I was in a daze, but mixed with the sense of sheer apathy was the incessant pounding in my head of the words "I must overcome. I must overcome . . ." The camp fence appeared, and we threw the wood down in front of the SS barracks, so that they could have heat for their quarters and enjoy a warm bath. When I took off my "shoes" in the shed, my feet were swollen and blue, and I could no longer feel my toes. Everything seemed numb. I rubbed my feet like one demented, so that I could at least, after half an hour, feel the pain that told me that I still had some life left in my limbs.

While in Camp IV, amid all our misery and in the throes of despair, we again tried to become active as ABC men. There were a number of members from the underground movement in Kaunas in this camp, and so we were able to establish contacts with one another and speak Hebrew amongst ourselves. It began gradually, not at any particular point in time. We did not make a conscious decision to re-form as a group; rather, we met with one another, and by discussing literature and other subjects, we managed to maintain our human dignity in the face of hunger and degradation. We could not allow ourselves to lose heart or abandon the hope that this hell would one day come to an end. Our talks with the others, of course, revolved almost exclusively around food. It got to the point where I had real hallucinations about food. My greatest desire was always a cup of cocoa and a piece of farmers bread with lots of butter and cheese — which we used to get during our vacations in the country, or which my mother bought in Kaunas at the farmers market. As the youngest in our family, I had been spoiled by my parents and aunts and often received what I wanted — cocoa, chocolate, whatever I fancied. I could now only dream about these mouth-watering delicacies.

In Camp IV we all worked — my father, my brother, and I — in the underground aircraft factory. For a while my father even directed a small work group, thanks to his professional experience. He was, after all, a specialist in that field. I was very glad for him, since this meant he did not have to carry the ton-heavy train rails or iron bars. He was then around forty-seven years old, my brother was twenty-one, and I, eighteen. Up until then we had been together the whole time, and this human bond made the task of survival all the more personal and urgent. But then my father fell seriously ill and had to go to the infirmary. He had a prostate condition, and a doctor who was a friend of ours from Lithuania tried to help him by inserting a needle into his abdomen, in order to get through to the bladder and free the urinary tract. By then, however, my father had already gotten blood poisoning, and his condition became hopeless. The poisoning made him delirious in the last hours of his life, and he did not even recognize his sons. My brother and I kept vigil by his bedside and refused to believe that after our mother we would also have to lose our father. He could not be saved and finally died in my arms. Now only my brother and I were left.

Shortly afterwards I also ended up in the infirmary. I had a serious lung infection and a high fever. During this time, as I lay on a wooden bed, covered only in a couple of old, rough blankets, my brother came one day to me and told me that young people, who could still work well, were being transferred to another camp. We both hoped that he would not be included, so that we could stay together. But he and four of his friends were assigned to the next transport, and we had to separate. When we parted we embraced and promised each other to meet after the war in Palestine. We had a cousin there, and we wanted to see each other again as soon as possible. We had to survive, so that we could again build up a new family with our name in Palestine. The idea of revenge was also involved in this decision: We wanted to be stronger than our enemies, who had set themselves the goal of annihilating us. By no means could we allow them this victory. Our victory over them, our revenge, would be our survival.

My brother waved to me once more as he departed and winked at me knowingly, as if wanting to remind me of our promise, as he and his friends were taken to the railway station to be transported to Leibmoritz. The prisoners were to work there in an armaments factory.

Sick and starving, I found myself totally alone in Camp IV. My father and my mother were dead, and my brother had left for an unknown fate. With increasing frequency, I found myself thinking, What is the point of all this? But just as quickly the counter-er reaction flashed in my mind: I will meet my brother again, I must survive, this is our revenge. The conviction that I had to survive gave me strength and the will to live.

This conviction stayed with me right up until liberation. I did not know then that I would be the only survivor of my family and that I would never meet my brother again. A survivor who was with my brother and his friends in the same camp, and whom I later met among displaced persons in Frankfurt, told me after the war about my brother's death. My brother, his friend Jatkunsky, and two others did escape from the camp. But a few days later they were caught and executed by the Germans.

After my father's death and my brother's departure I had no more close friends in Camp IV, not even the former members of the ABC. We were constantly being transferred to other camps, shoved here and there. I was alone, helpless, and lonely.

Shortly after these events I was taken to External Camp V, where the situation was decidedly worse than in Camp IV. Next to the men's camp there was also a women's camp, where the women, mostly Hungarian, were trying to survive. Their lot was somewhat better than ours, in terms of food. Their kitchen was situated near the fence that separated the two camps. Each of us tried to get some of the "culinary treasures" near the fence from the neighboring women — bread, potato peels, and perhaps even a potato. One Hungarian woman had seen me there near the fence, and I must have aroused her maternal instincts, because she supplied me for a while with pieces of bread and a potato from time to time. The woman called me "Kischkokosch," and the other Hungarian women always laughed when she called me by this name. When I finally found out what it meant, I also had to laugh. "Little rooster" was her nickname for me. When, after the war, I trotted out the few Hungarian words this woman had taught me, those listening always smiled. I'd say, "Budapest is a nice city, and the little rooster will have a look at it." Many years later, the not-so-little rooster actually did have the opportunity to visit Budapest.

I was in Camp V for only a short time. I can barely remember my stay there. However, the time I spent in Camp VII, the dreaded typhus camp, where I was taken with my friend Jascha after Camp V, is engraved in my memory. Half of the prisoners were in quarantine, and the other half had either been released from, or were waiting to be put into, quarantine.

In February 1945, I was transferred to the sick

camp or, more accurately, death camp. The human wrecks who could no longer work were brought to this camp, where they received even less to eat. After a few days, most of them were so weak that they could not move their bodies at all; they lay apathetically on the wooden boards and waited for their death or liberation. A few recovered and registered themselves for various jobs in the camp, and would be rewarded with food. But for the most part, the men were suffering from dysentery or typhus. The lice diligently carried the typhus from one prisoner to another. The disease started with a sudden fever and headache. The fever frequently rose to 42 degrees Celsius — about 107 Fahrenheit. During the night, delirious skeletons staggered around the camp like ghosts, looking for long-dead relatives. Many froze, some longed to join their relatives in the death chamber. We always found them dead the next morning, under the water tap. Really we should have held onto them somehow, but the healthy ones had to sleep during the night, so they would not themselves soon be added to the number of dead. Sleep was as precious as food.

Jascha and his father also contracted typhus after a few days in this camp. They were immediately sent to the quarantine section, but I always came to the sick block to make sure they got something to eat. I provided them with watery soup or potato peels and in this way I kept them alive. Jack, as Jascha calls himself today, still remembers these "deliveries" and claims that I saved his life in this manner. In the ghetto, conversations had been sufficient to give us encouragement; now we needed potato peels. But it was not only food that made the difference between life or death, it was our determination more than anything. Only the determination to keep on going gave us the willpower to survive this hell.

Yet from one day to the next it became more difficult. People in Camp VII were dying like flies, and every day the heap of bodies rose higher with the additional corpses. The sick lay naked under filthy blankets, mostly three to a bed. They rubbed themselves on the plank bed and after a few days could no longer roll from one side to another. It was hard to say which was the worst: the back that was raw from scratching, the illness itself, or the lice, which fell on the sick in droves and began sucking the blood from their veins. These tiny creatures were two to three millimeters in size, wingless, and crawled on their three pairs of legs among the sick. Their menu in the camp consisted of human blood, which they got in abundance from the prisoners. It was above all those who had typhus who suffered considerably from the loss of blood. But that wasn't all: These small insects also sucked out the typhus bacillus with the blood, and carried it through their excrement to the next sick person, whose bloodstream they ravaged. The lice multiplied at an astonishing rate, as did the number of prisoners with typhus. There was almost no hope of escaping the combination of the two.

It was in the midst of this situation when I first became aware of the full scope of the insanity that was going on. Outside it was spring: The sun was shining and the birds were chirping. I asked myself how all of this could possibly be: Everything is green and blooming in all its splendor, nature is following its normal course, most people are leading ordinary lives, and we are dying in a camp governed by suffering. In the face of this I asked myself, 'Is there a God? And if there is, how can he tolerate this?' I was angry with a God who could permit the incineration of people and the murdering of babies.

One encounter I remember from that time was with a French doctor who came with a transport of five hundred underground fighters from the Resistance. He was a Jewish doctor and always examined the sick, under instructions from the Germans. He had to decide who should go to quarantine and who was still fit for work. When he examined me I was already infected with typhus, but he hid the fact, and I was not forced to go to the dreaded sick block. An SS guard came over and said to him: "This one is finished." But the doctor turned to me and ordered: "Stand up! Stand up!"

I stood up, and he replied to the soldier, "No, he is healthy."

On the strength of this we became friends. I had learned French in school, so we were able to converse. I still count him among those who helped me remain alive.

Many years later at the Frankfurt Book Fair in Germany, I met a Mrs. Mélsine Tilsit, from Germany, who was married to a French Jew. We had a mutual publisher friend in Paris, and we met for dinner during my next stay in Paris. Her husband introduced himself during our conversation. He told me that his father had also been sent in the winter of 1944–1945 to Camp VII in Kaufering. He was brought there with fighters from the Resistance. I became very attentive when I heard this. I told him about the French doctor whom I had met in the camp. He became very excited, as his father had been a doctor. The next day he immediately set about trying to find out whether there had been other doctors in the French group. After checking, he found out that indeed only one doctor had accompanied this transport, and this was his father. And so he learned through me about his father's last days, about his integrity and warm-hearted character. I did not know that this doctor had died a few days later in the camp, and that our encounter had been one of the last of his life.

In Camp VII there were only "Musselmen" left in the end, living skeletons who could carry out the only camp work: taking corpses to the crematorium and burying them. Nonetheless, roll call was still carried out every day until shortly before liberation.

One morning the alarm was sounded in the camp. For a while we had been able to observe that something was wrong with the Germans. All those of sound limb were brought to the assembly square,

as well as the inmates from the women's camp.
This signaled the beginning of the evacuation.

6

LIBERATION

YEARS OF HOPE

Duaring this time, the camp saw the arrival of many transports with prisoners who looked more dead than alive. They had grown as thin as skeletons, and it was only a matter of days or even hours before they took their leave of this world. They told us of the death marches they had survived, the forced movement from one camp to another to evade the liberating armies. The Kapos had become more and more savage, beating them at every opportunity. If an SS guard got angry at a prisoner, he would take his hat, throw it away, and order him to fetch it. When the victim went to get the hat, the SS man shot him in the back and claimed that he had tried to escape. Sometimes they would shatter a prisoner's jaw, which was essentially an execution, since the injured prisoner could no longer eat and was dead within a few days.

In the second half of April, almost all the inmates of our camp were also sent on a death march. We could already hear the shots from the approaching Allied front. I told my friend Schimek, a young Pole from Lodz who'd been in the same block with me in Camp VII: "Listen, we are too weak, we will not survive the march. Let's hide here in the camp."

In the general chaos that prevailed, we hurried to our makeshift shed and hid there. We buried ourselves underneath the straw and hoped that they would not search the sheds again. But the Germans had something else planned. After the prisoners left the camp, they set everything on fire. The smoke that wafted in from the outside filled my nose, and I recognized the danger. We had to get out right away if we didn't want to suffocate or burn to death. I shouted at Schimek: "Come on, quickly, get out of here! Or we will be burned!" But he was already so apathetic he did not move. He couldn't care anymore. I roared at him again, and then dragged him out of the shed with me on all fours. Using our last ounce of strength, we dragged ourselves to a fence that was no longer protected by guards. My only thought was how to get my jacket off and use it to pull apart the fence so that we could crawl through. And then I saw soldiers approaching us. They looked different from SS men. They wore unfamiliar uniforms and drove vehicles that I had never seen before. These were American soldiers in jeeps. We were liberated! It was April 27, 1945.

The few survivors in the men's camp ran out from their hiding places; there were more prisoners in the women's camp who had been able to save themselves. Everyone ran outside looking for something edible. They ransacked the storehouse that the Germans had abandoned in such a hurry and poked here and there looking for some food. I didn't join in the search, but just sat there, devastated, in a corner. An American officer noticed me and came over. I was able to speak to him in broken English, and he wanted to know why I was so sad, despite the fact that we were now free. My answer was: "Look at me. Why should I be happy? My parents are dead, I have no home, I am alone and nothing makes sense anymore." My words must have moved him, for he immediately took me to his jeep and brought me to an American military field hospital in Bad Wörishofen.

After what I had experienced in the camp, I was both physically and mentally depleted. My body was covered with festering sores caused by hunger and typhus, and I weighed only thirty-three kilos. As I was taken up the hospital stairs on a stretcher, we passed by a long mirror. By chance I saw my reflection, and what I saw shocked me. I could barely see out of my swollen eyes, but I could not connect what I saw there with my own person. Who was this skeleton? It could not be me, the healthy, energetic young man from Kaunas who had always managed to grab the basketball from the big boys.

In the hospital I was placed in a bathtub with Caliumpermangane, a red disinfecting agent, in order to clear my body of the abscesses. The attending personnel and doctors were constantly trying to relieve me of my precious treasures — a plate and a spoon—but I would not let them out of my hand. Without these two objects one could not have survived in the camp, and I could not quite accept that other circumstances now prevailed. It required tremendous effort to convince me that I would be given food even without these objects. Only gradually did I begin to absorb the fact that I no longer had to fear for my ration. When I was led to a soft bed with white cotton sheets I was completely bewildered: I sat helplessly on the bed and did not know how I should lie down — with my head first on the bed, or with my legs? I was totally helpless and tried them both at the same time.

The sheets had to be replaced frequently, since my abscesses ruptured and were constantly draining. I lay in my bed, floating between dream and wakefulness — everything was foggy. Suddenly I heard voices near me and saw two American officers with two German officers who were probably doctors. As I opened my eyes, the first thing I noticed was a white robe and underneath it the feared boots of a German officer. Half dreaming, I heard the voice of the American officer complaining to the German doctor, "See what you have done!" I heard how the one right near me said to the other in German, "This case is hopeless!"

His words stabbed me like a knife. I was completely confounded: Now, when I'm lying in a soft bed with white sheets, I'm supposed to be a hopeless case? Out of the blue, I screamed: "You are hopeless! This case is not hopeless! This case is going to live."

This experience gave me back my old obstinate will. The power to survive had returned. Within a short time I recovered and my condition improved rapidly. I soon found the strength to stand up and move my legs. The nurses fed me with small portions of semisolid food, helping me to get used to normal food slowly. In spite of this, from time to time I stole a small piece of bread from the bread cart that stood in the corridor, and placed it under my pillow. Only then could I fall asleep. For a long time I used to sleep with a piece of bread under my pillow. Time just had to take its course before I could return to normal life.

But I made rapid progress and soon regained my health. The American officer who had brought me to the hospital came to visit me after a week. He picked me up and simply brought me to his unit. I was to work there as a translator. From then on he looked after me personally, and I became like an adopted son for him. I was given a U.S. Army uniform and was treated like one of the soldiers. I was now among normal, young, healthy Americans, who were all friendly and ready to help. We understood each other very well and acted quite natural with one other. They had experienced the war and seen much suffering — as I had. This created a kind of bond between us. I was a sort of mascot for them.

My English improved in a very short time. I

read the American troops' newspaper, *Stars and Stripes,* and soon I was able to hold lengthy conversations in English with little effort. With German, English, Russian, and some French I could be of assistance to the unit and also to the individual soldiers. I was one of them.

After a while our unit was transferred from Bad Wörishofen to Falkenau in Czechoslovakia. The place lay near the border between the Soviet and the American zones. Here I could help the Americans near the border with Russia. There was a thriving business in souvenirs with the Russian soldiers. For example, one could exchange a watch for a machine gun. Naturally, cigarettes were also much sought after by the Russian soldiers.

During this time, thousands of people were crossing Europe in transit. Many refugees and "displaced persons," or DPs, wanted to return to their homes and countries; others wanted to leave as quickly as possible. Jewish refugees tried to enter the American zone from the east and from there travel to Palestine. One day I was called to the railway station in order to translate for a trainload of displaced persons, since the Americans did not know how to communicate with the two people in charge. They spoke an entirely unknown language. When I arrived at the railway station, I saw two young men talking. I drew nearer and heard that they were speaking Hebrew. I caught some parts of the conversation. "You have to be careful with this one," said one of them, pointing at me. "They have brought him here especially because of us. No doubt he is here for a special purpose."

They took me for an American. They had accompanied the train that had come illegally from the Russian zone into the American zone, and were now worried that they might have to go back. I went over to them and said in Hebrew: "You don't have to be afraid of me! I am one of you."

I discovered after a while that these two were from Palestine, members of the Jewish Brigade, which accompanied trains that came illegally from Poland, Russia, and other countries into the American zone. Officially, they were en route as English soldiers of the Jewish Brigade, who had fought in Europe during the war. Unofficially, they were members of the Haganah, the Jewish underground movement in Palestine, and were now trying to arrange transports of Jewish refugees to the American zone, later to be sent on through Italy or France to Palestine. Since the end of the war, I had had very little contact with Jewish survivors, given that there had only been a few Jews in Bad Wörishofen. This, then, was how my involvement with Aliya Bet — the illegal immigration to Palestine — came into being.

We let the train continue on its way unhindered, and I explained the situation to our commanding officer. He immediately ordered that trains with Jewish DPs be allowed through without inspection and that in the future, I should be notified immediately about the arrival of such trains. Since I was named William in my unit, these trainloads were now called "William's people." In this way Falkenau became an important crossing point for Jewish immigrants en route to their new homeland. I soon established the necessary contacts, and after a short time I always received news, one or two days in advance, that a new group of arrivals was expected. We could even prepare tea, coffee, and something to eat, so that the DPs could at least be provided with the bare necessities.

Having been renamed William instead of Wulik by the Americans, I soon acquired another nickname: "William-jam-'n'-butter." As a regular soldier I naturally also had to do KP duty like any other soldier, peeling potatoes or whatever else was needed. Each morning, huge pots of food would be placed on the long table for breakfast, and the attending kitchen personnel had to distribute the contents to the soldiers. One morning the mess sergeant called to me, "William, you take the jam and butter." Since I was not familiar with this breakfast combination and wanted to do the soldiers a favor, I set the butter on the stove, warmed it slightly and, trying to be efficient, mixed it with the marmalade, to save the soldiers the effort of doing it themselves. They were more than a little surprised when I handed out the new spread. The line moved forward and in response to each one's request — whether for butter only, or jam only — I announced, "Today we have jam and butter," and before they could reply, the new mixture was plunked onto their plates. There was great laughter, and my new nickname was born.

After a few months our unit was supposed to leave Falkenau, and the army unit was shipped back to the States. This inevitably raised the question of my future. In the meantime the commanding officer who had taken me to the hospital in his jeep had grown very fond of me. He had no children of his own and cared for me as if I were his son. He wanted me to go with him to the States, but though I liked him very much, I already had other plans.

Shortly before the unit was to be shipped back to the States, General George Patton appeared in our camp for an inspection. He had been informed about me and my work for the unit, and I was introduced to him. He wanted to know briefly about my past and then told me that I could join the unit and be shipped back with them to the States. I ventured to make a request: "General, I would prefer to go to Palestine."

He looked at me in surprise. "Why Palestine?"

"I want to go there to help the Jews get their own state. They should be able to live like other people in their own country."

"But Jews live freely in the United States and elsewhere, why do you need Palestine?"

"What happened in Europe should never be allowed to happen again, sir."

"But who will give you this state? Palestine is under British mandate!"

"If necessary," I answered with determination,

"we'll have to fight for it!"

He seemed to like my forceful reply, because he responded in a commanding tone: "Then fight for it! Go ahead, go, go!"

I could only answer gratefully: "Yes, sir. Thank you, General!"

Saying good-bye to my American patron, who had already notified his wife that he was bringing me with him, was very painful for us both. I tried as best I could to present to him my reasons: that I definitely had to go to Palestine to meet my brother again, that we had to work on the building of our own state, that I could not abandon my dreams for liberation. I could not just pick up and leave behind me the horror of the camps and the murder of the Jews to go to what was for me an entirely foreign country, and sit back and enjoy life there. I wanted a place I could call my own, of which I could feel proud. Although it was difficult for him to understand my reasons, he accepted my decision.

The unit was taken to an abandoned airstrip near Frankfurt, before the final journey back to the States. A tent town was built there for us, and I used the opportunity to arrange a pass for Frankfurt. I wanted to reestablish contacts with the people from Palestine who were taking care of the illegal immigration and had taken on the task of organizing the journey further on. All my contacts up until now had been disrupted by the short-term transfer of our troops, and I wanted to renew these connections as soon as possible.

One morning I traveled to Frankfurt in the hope of finding there the place that handled the transports of Jewish refugees. I wandered from one authority to the next, went to the American and then to the German municipal administration, but no one could give me any further information. At last I was directed to an institution in Wiesenhüttenstrasse. After searching for hours I finally arrived at Wiesenhüttenstrasse. It was already late afternoon, and I had almost lost hope of finding such an aid organization. But as it turned out I was in precisely the right place. I entered a small office, and as I went into the room, the man present immediately stood up, since I was wearing my American military uniform. Speechless, we stared at one another for a few seconds. We knew each other. He was Yitzhak Ratner, from my hometown of Kaunas, who had also been active in the Zionist movement. The secretary, Dita Appel, also a native of Kaunas, remembered me as well. The two were surprised at my uniform, and I briefly told them my story. Dita's husband, Manfred Simon, came in shortly afterwards. During the war they had lost each other and had begun searching for one another immediately after liberation. Luckily they succeeded. Soon afterwards, they moved to Frankfurt after the city authorities were obliged to allocate apartments to former residents. Since Manfred had been born in Frankfurt, they now had a place on Schneidheimerstrasse. We talked about the organization and its activities. In this way I was able to reestablish my contacts with the illegal immigration to Palestine, Aliya Bet.

Manfred and Dita were more than friendly; there was mutual affection from the outset, and they treated me like family — which we later became. We decided that I should leave my unit and move in with them. Who would have thought that I would move in with my future sister-in-law and brother-in-law? Dita, who had no great culinary experience, tried out her fledgling cooking skills on us, and we were able to survive the experiments with humor.

When I arrived at their apartment, I noticed on the mantelpiece a picture of a young girl with black ringlets. She looked at me through her soft almond-shaped eyes, and I asked Manfred, "Who is this, then?"

"That is my sister. She is with our mother in the DP camp in Feldafing on Lake Starnberg."

"So when does she usually come to visit?"

Manfred smiled and said, "She herself isn't coming, but my mother will arrive here in a few days."

My encounter with Manfred's mother was indeed something extraordinary. Not for a long time had I met such an intelligent, warmhearted, and interesting woman. She reminded me very much of my own mother: liberal-minded and ready to help, educated, and extremely charming. We became friends at first sight. She was very glad to meet someone who could speak with her so well in German and who shared the same interests. We both liked the opera, and I sang to her some of the arias that had stayed in my memory since Kaunas. We also had extremely lively talks about literature for hours, and I felt an unbelievable sense of well-being in her company. As a result of her stay in the camps she had lost the vision in one eye, underwent surgery, and lost the eye. But she still had a penetrating gaze, which seemed to touch the core of my soul.

When she left I promised her: "If your daughter Trudi comes to Frankfurt sometime, I'll take her to the theater or the opera." She seemed to like this idea, for she smiled meaningfully as she boarded the train to Munich. Some time was to pass before I had this opportunity.

❖

Through my contacts with the Halutzim, the pioneers in Geringshoff, I got to know someone who became one of my best friends — Herbert Growald. We worked with the Jewish Agency, the shadow government of the Jewish state about to be established, a body representing the interests of the Jews living in Palestine, and a connecting link between Jews in the Diaspora and in Palestine. His girlfriend at the time — later his wife — Aliza, had escaped during the war from Germany to England and returned with the British army after the war had ended. She was likewise very active in our immigration activities. The couple later had an apartment in Friedrichstrasse, where the Aliya Bet office was located.

This apartment was also where I met David Ben-Gurion for the first time, in 1946. He had come to Germany in order to visit the DP camps and get an idea of the situation. It was not an official political visit. He had fled the English, who had wanted to arrest him for his activities with the Jewish Agency. During his stay in Germany he was taken care of by us, so he also visited the house in Friedrichstrasse where I was working for Aliya Bet. We spoke in Hebrew, and he asked me from which kibbutz in Palestine I had come (the kibbutzim were known for their involvement in Aliya Bet activities). I answered, "I am not a kibbutznik."

"But neither do you look like someone who comes from Tel Aviv," he replied.

My answer was: "I don't come from Tel Aviv. I myself am a DP."

I explained to him that I was from Kaunas and had learned Hebrew there in the Hebrew high school. Afterwards we retired into a small adjacent room, he closed the door behind us and asked me to tell him my story. He questioned me for hours and wanted to know everything about me. Years later, when we met again in Israel at some official function, he could still remember me and our conversation in Frankfurt.

Around this time I also met someone else. Trudi was finally scheduled to visit her brother in Frankfurt, and I was already very anxious. Naturally I did not betray my interest, but arranged things so that I was at the railway station "by chance" when the train arrived with her and her uncle, who had come as her chaperone. Manfred and Dita were very surprised to see me there. I sauntered as casually as possible into the station building, and there she stood: a young girl, plump, in a nice dress and white patterned stockings up to her knees. Although she was seventeen years old, she had the facial expression of a sweet fourteen- or fifteen-year-old. I greeted her, took the bag she was holding on her arm, and introduced myself as Zev Birger. I had made "Zev"— the Hebrew equivalent of Wulik — my first name after leaving the American unit, since I no longer saw any reason to be called William. We all boarded the streetcar to go to the apartment, and I used this opportunity to get to know her.

"You must be Trudi, Manfred's sister. I saw your picture at Manfred and Dita's and have heard so much about you," I began, and we immediately became involved in a lively conversation. She really got enthusiastic when I asked her about her future plans.

"We're all going to America, the whole family. My mother, Manfred, Dita, and I. We only have to wait for the documents," she informed me.

"You are not going to America," I said to her

very decisively.

"Why not then? Everything is already prepared!"

"You are going to Palestine."

"Why Palestine? What am I going to do there?"

"You are going to go with me!"

"And why should I go with you?" She looked at me strangely.

"You will go with me, indeed — as my wife!"

With that, Trudi was left completely speechless.

I could not explain it to myself, but I had this feeling of absolute certainty that she would become my wife. It all just fit: the picture at Dita and Manfred's, the mother who had captured my heart, and our first meeting in the railway station, which had taken place less than half an hour earlier.

She was truly at a loss for words, but I could see by her look that she thought I was crazy. I could well understand it. But this young girl was like her mother: She was clever, cultured, and warmhearted, and she knew what she wanted. I was now absolutely certain that she was the right one for me, and that I would do everything to convince her of this.

She proved that she had a head on her shoulders that very evening. She was invited together with Dita and Manfred to the Jewish Welfare Board, and since she knew no one, she decided to leave early. Although she was as good as lost in Frankfurt and didn't know her way around at all, she simply got on the streetcar. She did remember one point of reference — the police station — but she missed the stop. She got out at the wrong spot, which did not upset her too much, because she was certain that she would soon find the house in Schneidheimer-strasse. But at this time of night there was not a soul on the streets: it was dark and also quite dangerous. When Manfred and Dita got home they asked me in complete surprise where Trudi was. She should have been home half an hour earlier. So we immediately started a search. Dita and Manfred went in one direction and I went in the other. Luckily, fate had it that I was the one to find her, and secretly she was no doubt glad about this as well. She smiled at me and said that she had been absolutely sure she was going in the right direction. I accompanied her home and made her promise to avoid such nightly escapades in future. We spent the rest of her stay in Frankfurt together, taking long walks, going to the theater and movies, and talking for hours. After a week she returned to her mother in Feldafing, and I had the feeling that saying good-bye was as hard for her, maybe even harder, as for me. We were in love. From then on I also made it a habit to take that streetcar, whenever I could manage it.

My activities in Aliya Bet took me all over Europe. I drove from one DP camp to another, organized groups of young Jews, and helped prepare them for the journey to Palestine. Teachers and instructors were sent from Palestine, mostly from the Haganah, who taught the camp survivors Hebrew, the basics of agriculture, Israeli folk songs, and self-defense. The main task of our organization was to transport the former camp inmates to ports on the Mediterranean, and from there to boats that took them further, to Palestine.

Our work in the DP camps was well-organized and progressed smoothly. This next stage in the journey of the Jewish immigrants was prepared in the camps. There we knew about the exact number of people who wanted to go, and we had to make this number tally with the number of places available on the ships that were leaving Italy or France. It was a big network, and we, in Frankfurt, were only one of the centers. The minute we got word that a group was about to arrive, we prepared trains, and got beverages and something to eat ready at the railway station. Besides that, we of course organized the continuation of the journey and, where necessary, the overnight arrangements for those who had to spend one or more nights in Frankfurt.

The vehicles, as well as the petrol, that we needed were often put at our disposal by the American military. But mostly we had to organize things on our own. Sometimes this was a slow and difficult process, and we had to invent some tricks to allow us to carry out the transports quickly and smoothly. After all, we couldn't afford to have a traffic jam. It was like a game of dominoes. The first domino had just fallen and we had to make sure that the rest of the row fell, too. The refugees who came to us needed papers that would secure their passage out of Germany as well as the journey beyond. In order to acquire these permits, I have to admit we made good use of the pandemonium that prevailed at the time. We got travel visas to South American countries for five hundred to one thousand persons, and with these visas we went to the headquarters of the American forces in Frankfurt, in order to obtain the exit permits as well as the transit permits for the journey through the French zone.

We drew up lists of names with the help of telephone books. We then had these lists stamped at the headquarters and also asked for a stamped copy — supposedly for our own documents. But in fact we used both the original and the copy and set up two different transports using the same list, one by train and one via trucks or other vehicles. This way we could quickly get twice the number of refugees out of the country.

Often, it was all more fiction than fact. A lot depended on how well one could bluff. One of our drivers in Frankfurt, Alfred Steier, was very good at this game. He was a German who had been sent to a concentration camp for being a Social Democrat. Whenever we had to deal with the authorities he addressed me as "Doctor," and also introduced me with this title. This was indeed very brash; given my twenty years, American uniform, and youthful appearance I did not exactly look like an academic with a doctoral degree. But he tried to reason with me, saying, "Zev, in Germany, if you are not a doctor, you are nothing." It was the quickest degree I ever earned.

The splitting up of the various Zionist organizations did not make our work simpler. For example, what was left of the ABC organization set up a new Zionist party, Noham, which had an extremely naive ideology — to establish a unified Zionist organization with the goal of building up the land in Palestine and gaining an independent state. But Noham was worn down by the existing parties and dissolved quickly.

There was tremendous confusion in those days. This was, of course, not surprising, since many survivors were disoriented and did not even know where to go. Most of them had been saved from the concentration camps — in some cases directly from the incinerators — and had lost everything: families, property, homeland. Many tried to return to their original homes, but Europe was in a shambles and nothing remained as before. Where were their old friends, old hopes, and shared dreams?

Things were much easier for me than for most of the survivors. I had been taken in immediately after liberation by the U.S. military unit, a friendly group of people who treated me as an equal. Consequently, my transition to normal life was made much easier. Now that I was working with Aliya Bet, I was among young Israelis. I spoke their language, picked up their manners, looked and acted like one of them. I was never identified as a DP. So when I eventually arrived in Palestine, I was "almost Israeli," in total contrast to those who were closely packed together in the DP camps.

They had no chance of forgetting their past; their environment constantly reminded them of the last horrible years at the hands of the Nazis. They spoke all the time about their experiences of persecution, the atrocities in the ghetto and later in the concentration camps. Thus it was unavoidable that an atmosphere of hatred and revenge against the Germans prevailed in the DP camps.

I shared the view that it was unforgivable that Germany had followed Hitler since 1933 and plunged the world into a terrible war. The German people had brought about the wholesale extermination of Jews as well as other outcasts, whether actively or passively. But I had also met a few Germans who were anything but fanatic followers of the regime, like the AEG engineer who, despite adverse circumstances, maintained a degree of humanity and, in helping me, refused to go along with the mass insanity.

Nevertheless, even today I find it sometimes difficult to communicate with Germans of the prewar generation. The stereotypical response of "we knew nothing" is both unacceptable and untrue. I do, however, meet many Germans of the postwar generations who have developed a marked awareness regarding German history, and with whom I can share my thoughts about the past. For years after the war I developed personal contacts with the younger generations of Germans. I saw it as my duty to talk to them about their history and its consequences, so they will learn what happened and prevent it from happening again. Right after the war the Germans adopted a feigned submissive attitude, ostensibly an 180-degree turnaround. However, during my work in Frankfurt and also much later, I met many Germans with whom I really enjoyed working. I soon came to the conclusion that it's not the difference between nations that is significant, but rather the gulf between good and bad people within different nations. If one were to judge the Germans solely by nationality, one would be following a Nazi ideology, which could — in the worst scenario — lead to crimes similar to those that had been perpetrated against the Jews, who were first condemned as a people and a race.

But what troubled me was the fact that too many people had been living like the proverbial three monkeys — seeing, hearing, and speaking no evil. They had turned off their minds and their reason, so they would not have to assume any responsibility for their country's actions. This is one of the points that I hope will be preserved in the young generation's memory. One should not forget what can happen when one gives free rein to extremism and fails to oppose intolerance, or racial or religious discrimination. None of this was an issue between Alfred, our German driver in Frankfurt, and myself. We visited each other and were simply friends. We were two people who had been through a lot, and did not judge each other on the basis of origin. The most important thing is remembering. I don't think that I can or should ever forgive what was done in those years. We must keep the memory of it alive and try to prevent similar crimes from being perpetrated again.

Dita and Manfred managed to book their passage to the United States in early 1946. The visa for Trudi and her mother had not yet arrived, and they moved into the Frankfurt apartment with us while they waited for the papers. But they had not yet made any final arrangements. I noticed that I had infected the two women with my enthusiasm for Palestine, and they were no longer so sure that they should go to the United States.

My Zionist studies were now able to bear fruit. Trudi's mother had already demonstrated her commitment to Zionism earlier. I built my arguments on that foundation. They weighed at length the pros and cons of a journey to Palestine, which at the time would clearly not be a step toward an easy life. At the beginning of 1946, there was still no United Nations resolution for partition, and certainly no declaration of independence on the part of Israel. This was to come about only on May 8, 1948. But in the end I was able to convince Mrs. Simon that the Jews belonged in their own country and we should go to Palestine to live in our rightful home, and not as foreigners elsewhere. I believe that Mrs. Simon had been persuaded early on that I was the right man for her daughter. She realized how well suited we were, and that it would be best for all of us if we continued together on our future path. For that reason she was particularly receptive to my arguments for emigration to Palestine. The debate, however, led to heated arguments with Dita and Manfred, who were very glad that the family would now finally be living together again in the States. But from April 1946, I worked hard to bring about the immigration to Palestine of Trudi, her mother, and myself. It was also at this point in time that Trudi and I found ourselves deeply and hopelessly in love, and we decided to get married. She had some reservations, including the fact that she was still so young and actually had missed out on her youth. She wanted to make something of herself, so had registered at Frankfurt University to study microbiology. But Trudi's love for me helped tip the scales in favor of emigrating to Palestine.

We had very happy times together in Frankfurt. I had a car, and so we went on trips and toured around the beautiful Rhine landscape. We visited historical sites in Germany—fortresses and castles were our favorite destinations. We often went together to a concert in the evening or allowed ourselves to be swept away by the melodies of the most popular operettas. We were amazed at how well we understood and complemented each other.

I often asked myself whether it was my late mother who had arranged all this for me. If she had still been with us, she certainly would have made the same choice. It was all so completely in keeping with her manner and her wishes for me. I believe that the blessing given to us by my mother in those last moments I saw her was fulfilled in my meeting Trudi.

We became engaged on June 1, 1946, and a month later we were married in the courtyard of the apartment building on Schneidheimerstrasse. It was a very simple celebration. Only the ten men required for prayer, as well as my mother-in-law and a couple of friends, were present. We invited mostly friends from Israel with whom I worked, a couple of friends from Geringshof, one or two members of the Frankfurt community, and the head of the Refugee Committee. We went to the American Jewish Welfare Board, where the wedding canopy stood, and were married by Captain Miller, a U.S. Army chaplain. It was unbelievable, but the entire time I had the feeling that my parents were also present and watching over my shoulder, smiling throughout the ceremony. I knew that in some way they were always with me, but never before had this struck me as profoundly as it did at our wedding. Never again was I to experience such an intense awareness of their presence.

After the ceremony we went to our apartment, and there a surprise was waiting for me. My mother-in-law had bought wine glasses and set the table beautifully. She must have gone to great effort and expense to come up with the dishes, embroidered tablecloth, and flowers. I was very moved. The meal was excellent, and in the afternoon coffee and cake were also served. We brought out a record player and started dancing waltzes, tangos, and

English waltzes. The mood was gay, even boister-
ous. I even received a present from my friends: a
cloth briefcase for my important work.

But my mother-in-law had another surprise
ready for us. We were to have a real honeymoon.
She had booked a room for us in a small guest
house in Taunus, where we spent a wonderful
week. The owner had even welcomed us with a
small sign on our door: "Welcome, Mr. and Mrs.
Birger." It took Trudi some time to realize that *she*
was actually "Mrs. Birger."

For breakfast we picked strawberries from the
fields, and the owner of the guest house gave us
whipped cream to have with them. It reminded me
of my family's vacations with the Lithuanian farmers. In the afternoon we'd go cherry picking, and as
a joke I hung paired cherries as earrings on Trudi's
small, pretty ears. We had an unbelievable craving
for fruit, since we had seen so little of it in the last
few years. When we got back to Frankfurt, my
mother-in-law also regularly bought fresh fruit for
me, so that I could get myself back into shape
healthwise. Camp existence had taken a visible toll
on my body.

When I think back after all these years, if some-
body were to ask me today how I would have liked
to celebrate my wedding and honeymoon, I would
answer: "The exact same way I celebrated in it
1946 in Frankfurt." I had found everything that my
heart desired: a wife I loved and who shared my
plans, a mother-in-law whom I liked and with

whom I shared a wonderful understanding. In Trudi and her mother I found the continuation of my own family, my past in Kaunas, and the happy days in our house near the city park.

At the end of 1946 the Zionist World Congress was held in Basel, as the first one had been in 1897. Our organization obtained travel documents for the delegates from Frankfurt. But when Herbert and I wanted to travel to Basel, there were problems with our own papers — we did not appear on the visa list. We decided to go with no papers, at least as far as Baden-Baden. So Herbert, Aliza, and I drove to Basel together with Captain Miller and his wife in an old Opel. Captain Miller had helped us get vehicles for the illegal emigration, and now he wanted to see for himself how one could cross the border without papers.

The car seat covers were no longer so new and actually quite shabby, so we threw military blankets over the seats. These blankets also fit in with our appearance, since we were all dressed as American officers. We passed the border between the American and the French zone uneventfully. Unlike Captain Miller, we were familiar with the route and knew roughly where the border lay. Near to where we assumed the border to be, we stopped at a farm and inquired about the way to the border. The farmer only said: "Ah, you have to drive back five kilometers." We could hardly help laughing when we looked at Captain Miller's surprised face. He had really not imagined it would be so easy.

So we arrived with no trouble at all in Baden-Baden, where our liaison waited for us with the documents. From there we headed out in the direction of the Swiss border. It was already nightfall and the rain was streaming down in rivers, so we could barely see the road. We had to stop somewhere if we didn't want to land in a ditch. In Bad Krozingen we noticed a small hotel right on the street. The dining room was full of French officers, who called out when we arrived, "Les camarades américains!" Herbert and I passed ourselves off as American officers and spoke only English in order to play it safe and avoid arousing suspicion. We were invited by them to eat, and of course there was also some drinking. We raised toasts to one another, and the mood grew increasingly relaxed. My friend Herbert, after a few glasses of wine, began to speak French. The French soon remarked to him: "Vous parlez très bien français." Naturally, this was not entirely in keeping with our disguise, but we got by without further incident, given the tipsy atmosphere. Nevertheless, we arose very early the next morning and left the hotel before our French comrades awakened — just in case they might remember the previous evening.

In a small village, shortly before reaching the Swiss border, we parted ways with Captain Miller and his wife. He still did not have the particular brand of self-confidence, even brashness — today one would call it chutzpah — with which we approached official places. We planned to meet again on the other side, since Herbert and I had to wait another couple of days for the liaison who would bring our other papers. In this little place, there was a tiny guest house, where we booked rooms. The owner had cleared out his barn and turned it into a movie theater. He also served beer there. So we sat between the troughs and the hay, drank beer, and watched Marlene Dietrich in *The Blue Angel*. We were every bit as enthralled as the villagers.

We crossed the border near Basel the next day and met Captain Miller on the other side. We then drove to the Zionist Congress. By dint of my arrival there I won a bet I had made with a friend, and was now the proud owner of fifty dollars. He had not believed that we would make it to Basel without any official documentation.

I was very impressed by the size of the assembly, and the array of participants who all had the same goal in their hearts: the establishment of a Jewish state. Dramatic Zionist speeches were made, and the enthusiasm was fantastic. We stayed for a few days and then drove back to Frankfurt.

In Basel I had bought something very important for my mother-in-law, an extraordinary luxury item that at the time almost no one possessed — a hot-water bottle. I decided that this was a very appropriate gift for her. She was a woman who radiated unbelievable warmth. One reason I felt so good in our apartment in Frankfurt was that it reminded me of the loving atmosphere in my childhood home. But I did not develop any personal attachment to the city and its residents. I knew that I was only in transit there and wanted to leave the country as soon as possible. Being very busy with my activity in the Jewish Agency, I barely had any time to prepare my own emigration.

But in August 1947 we were ready. We received permission to leave. The British had sharply curtailed the legal avenues of immigration, and immigrants could now reach the country only in small groups. So we developed a new code name: Aliya Daled (*daled* is the fourth letter in the Hebrew alphabet). The British usually apprehended the ships with illegal immigrants and held them in detention camps in Cyprus. We wanted to circumvent this by obtaining the papers of deceased persons from Palestine or of those who had "lost" their passports. We were supposed to pretend that we were returning from a European trip. But at first we had to stay for a few weeks in a DP camp in the British zone and wait for our papers. When these finally arrived, I was off to Marseilles. I was now Manu Birger, born 1919. I was a twenty-year-old man but held the passport of a woman, Mania, who was actually thirty years old. The first name and gender could be changed, but unfortunately nothing could be done about the birth date. But it was still better than having no papers at all.

In Marseilles, we boarded a ship called the *Aegean Star*, which had once been one of the Rothschild family's yachts. It was terribly small, and so we made very slow progress on our journey, but this did not spoil the mood on the ship. There were around two hundred passengers, among them our friends Herbert and Alisa Growald. Our captain was an older Greek man, with whom we quickly made friends. A real ladies' man, he immediately set his sights on Trudi. He was very disappointed when he realized that Trudi was married to me, but he was also a "good loser," inviting us to have dinner with him at the captain's table. There was a relaxed atmosphere on board, which did not let up during the two weeks of the trip. I also enjoyed teaching Alisa Growald a little Hebrew. I translated the words "I am pleased" to "Ani hamor" ("I am a donkey"), and each time she wanted to express her satisfaction, I could hardly contain my laughter. We had a lot of fun on board the ship, though we traveled under very cramped conditions. But it was nothing compared to the congestion in the camps. We sang Hebrew songs and formed friendships that have lasted to this day, fifty years later.

After nearly two weeks, the captain informed us that we would be within sight of Haifa the next morning. We stayed up the entire night, standing near the railings and gazing at the dark horizon. And then suddenly, still in the dark of night, someone spotted the lights of the port city, the lights of Jewish houses and streets.

At long last, after a wild journey through half of Europe, we had arrived in a land that was to be our home. My wife was trembling with joy next to me, and I also had tears in my eyes. Palestine—I had dreamed of it for such a long time, I had fought so hard. There it now lay before us, and I almost felt I'd have to jump overboard and swim the rest of the way, the ship was moving so slowly toward the shore. I was no longer worried about the future, my heart was full of joy and hope.

And so on November 20, 1947, I disembarked with my wife and mother-in-law. I held my loved ones tightly in my arms. Home at last! A place that was ours. No more wandering, no longer displaced. At last a new beginning and a new life!

7

JERUSALEM
FINALLY HOME

We arrived at my cousin Haim's place in Haifa. He had immigrated to Palestine before the war, and prior to our journey I found his address through the Jewish Agency and informed him about our travel plans. He came from a small town in Lithuania and had lived with us in Kaunas while pursuing his studies. I had originally hoped to find my brother with him, but, as I had heard from survivors in Leibmoritz, my brother and his friends had been shot after an attempted escape.

We found shelter with Haim and his family for a few days, but space was very limited, so we gladly accepted the offer of a friend of my mother-in-law's and moved in with her. It was in her apartment, anxiously sitting in front of the radio, that we heard the UN announce the decision to establish the State of Israel. We immediately ran down into the street and plunged into the throng of dancing, celebrating people. The mood on the streets was happy and high-spirited, as if we had already achieved everything we dreamed of. But, of course, we still had a long and treacherous path ahead.

We moved into our own apartment soon after. It was only a room where the three of us lived, but we were proud and glad to finally have a place of our own. We were to move several times in Haifa, but that first room on Mount Carmel has always held a special place in our hearts.

Now came the matter of finding work. I started my job hunt soon after our arrival. My cousin told me that the Customs Authority in Haifa was looking for a "junior clerk," and after making inquiries there, I managed to get a job working in the Manifest Department, which handled the cargo lists of the newly arrived ships. All of a sudden I found myself making the adjustment to a new routine; I had to get up every morning, go to work, and behave like a respectable citizen, slotting into a new society. Day-to-day life was now marked by issues of economic subsistence rather than basic survival. We needed to make friends and acquaintances to fit into this new framework. But I embarked on this new path with a sense of optimism, grateful to have the freedom to act and think without fear or constraints. The sights and sounds in the port were intoxicating. The hustle and bustle of Arab porters and foreign sailors—the smell of the oranges, fish, and machinery oil—all this was part of the busy, dizzying scene. In the midst of all this I felt a desire to breathe deeply, to embrace the world, to forge ahead in this new life.

I soon realized, however, that I had to look for additional work, because my pay at the Customs was nowhere near enough to support the three of us. I became a collector for an insurance company, often collecting premiums in areas of Haifa that lay further up Mount Carmel. I frequently carried out my work on foot, to save bus fare, and found myself climbing uphill on numerous occasions. These first years were very strenuous and full of deprivation, but we were tremendously enthusiastic and took all the inconveniences in stride without grumbling. My mother-in-law was also a great help — she baked cakes, which she sold to different cafés. We only had an oil burner on which to cook, but she got hold of a special tin box, the kind used in those days for baking cakes, and she made good use of it. Although the three of us had to share one room, we really did not have any problems getting along, even when times were anything but easy.

Following the UN declaration establishing the State of Israel, riots had broken out among the Arab population. As the months passed, there was increasing unrest, and it became more and more dangerous to drive down to the port. Soon we were using armored buses. When the War of Independence between the newborn State of Israel and its Arab neighbors broke out in May 1948, a bomb exploded near our office and caused considerable damage. The British had in the meantime left the country, and the battle for Palestine had begun. Like all young men, I was drafted and took part in the battles to liberate Haifa, in which I was wounded. The director of the Customs

Authority, who had left with the British, said to me before his departure, "Watch out, Birger. One day you will become the director of Customs."

As soon as I arrived in the country, I started making contacts with the Labor Party through the ABC group, and eventually became a member. But I was never an activist. I concentrated mainly on my work in the Customs Authority and my task as the chairman of the Customs Employees Union. Like many others I was also a member of the Histadrut Labor Federation, the main workers' union in the country.

I worked my way up over the years, until I did indeed become Customs director. Later, I sent my old friend a postcard in Cyprus, informing him that his prophecy had proved right. At the time, in 1957, this post was considered one of the most important in the Finance Ministry, as most of the country's revenue came from customs and excise. At that time, the government decided to transfer the headquarters of the Customs and Excise Authority to Jerusalem. This caused heated debate throughout the country. To most people a move from Haifa was unthinkable. After all, the port, as well as most of Israel's still fledgling industry, was in Haifa. If the Customs Authority was transferred, new apartments for the employees and employment for their wives or husbands would have to be found. There was a mountain of seemingly insurmountable problems. To add to all this, Jerusalem at the time was nothing more than a small town, and a divided town at that.

People often joked that everything shut down and the sidewalks folded up at eight o'clock at night.

Leaving Haifa was going to be difficult for us, too. We had bought a small house in Tivon, a Haifa suburb in the direction of Nazareth, with money we were able to raise from our reparations payments from Germany. The house was located about a half hour from Haifa in a beautiful location in the mountains. Our first son, Doron, and our second son, Oded, were born there. We could look at the sea from the large living-room window, and we had a nice garden. My wife had a good position as head of a medical laboratory, and my mother-in-law was also getting along extremely well. And we were supposed to give up all this in order to move to Jerusalem, a mere "village"? Most other families who were affected by the planned transfer felt the same way. Children were at school, people had jobs and felt at home. At the time, I should add, Haifa was considered a state within a state. Referred to as "Red Haifa," the city was a workers' center and had a great deal of political clout. We had influential politicians and union leaders who played a decisive role in the actions taken by the government.

So, for most of those involved, moving to Jerusalem was simply out of the question. Zeev Sharef, head of the Tax Authority and later the minister of industry and trade, tried to win me over to his side to support the move. As organizational director and acting Customs director, I would certainly have had a major influence on the employees, but at first I was also against the move. But deep down I already knew that the move was inevitable. When we had spoken about Palestine in the camps in Europe, we had been speaking and dreaming of Jerusalem — not Haifa. The city sung about in the Zionist songs was not Tel Aviv or Haifa, but Jerusalem, the Holy City. It was not only a city. It was a symbol — even if it was still a small, sleepy symbol.

But when he saw that I was still unwilling to speak out in favor of the move, Sharef arranged for me to be summoned by the finance minister, Levi Eshkol, in Jerusalem. This man had the habit of addressing everyone who was younger than himself as "young man." So there I was in front of him presenting my arguments, from a purely organizational point of view, against moving the Customs Authority to Jerusalem. I stressed that Haifa was still the largest port and that Jerusalem wasn't even anywhere near the sea. And then there was the problem of resettling families, and so on. After I had finished, he looked at me calmly and said: "Young man, with me you can argue. But King David decided almost three thousand years ago that Jerusalem should be the capital of Israel. So you have to take it up with him. The Central Customs Authority should certainly be in the capital of a country, shouldn't it?"

And to this I replied: "I can argue with you — but not with King David!

Given his straightforward and reasonable argument, I had no choice but to accept the decision. Ironically, as fate would have it, I would be given the task, almost exactly forty years later, of preparing the celebrations marking the three thousandth anniversary of the City of David.

I was made responsible for organizing the move, and from that time onward began working energetically at this task. More than two hundred people were moved from Haifa to Jerusalem. Special housing had to be constructed, and new jobs found for the spouses. In the first couple of months, many still had to commute daily between Haifa and Jerusalem or stay overnight in hotels. I made certain that every employee was fully informed of the particulars about his new place of work. When the people finally moved into their new offices they found everything perfectly organized and ready for work — from the waiting files to the flowers that greeted them on their desk. After the move, Jerusalem's stature noticeably increased. It was indeed a small, intimate city, but it grew. With the influx from Haifa, a huge economic upswing was set in motion.

At first my family lived in a hotel, the President Hotel in Rehavia, whose bar was the center of Jerusalem's entire nightlife. There were also a couple of other bars and cafés, but Jerusalem was a divided city, a border city. One was conscious of that border wherever one went. The Knesset, the Israeli parliament, was at the time still located on

King George Street, in the heart of downtown. But the face of Jerusalem was changing. With the Customs Authority move, hundreds of new jobs were generated in Jerusalem. All those who had dealings with the Customs Authority also came to Jerusalem. New bank branches opened, and additional administrative buildings sprang up. The city came to life.

Our family quickly adjusted to living in the capital of the young state. It was clear to us from the outset that we did not want to move into a housing complex or huge apartment block. In Beit Hakerem, a neighborhood on the city's outskirts, we found a pretty old house belonging to the widow of Professor Cherikover, known for his scholarly research on the Maccabees. Following his death the house had become too big for her, and she wanted to sell it. The house had a large, colorful garden, which was ideal for our two sons. In fact when I finally asked my older son how he liked the house, all he said was, "The garden is great."

Although the tax director, Sharef, thought my intention to buy this old dilapidated house — which was more expensive than the most luxurious apartments in the center of Jerusalem — was misguided, to say the least, we nonetheless decided to move to Beit Hakerem. There we could withdraw into the tranquillity of our garden, enjoy the shade of the high trees and the magnificent colors of the flower beds. With the help of an architect friend from Tel Aviv, we renovated the interior rooms, so that they were appropriate for a family with two children and a mother-in-law. We were quite happy with the results. From the outside the house did look old, but inside it was very comfortable. We soon made friends in Jerusalem and settled in nicely. My wife got a position as head of the laboratory at the General Health Clinic in Beit Hakerem. Shortly after moving in we once again began inviting over our friends and acquaintances on a regular basis.

A decisive advantage that Jerusalem had over Haifa was its cultural life, which was constantly developing and growing. There were more cultural activities, lectures, and concerts here. And on occasion the Israel Philharmonic also performed.

At the beginning of the 1960s, I attended the trial of Adolf Eichmann. A notorious SS officer, Eichmann had been one of the architects and key implementers of the extermination of European Jewry for the German Reich. As chief of operations, he had been instrumental in determining the pace and timing of deportations to the death camps. After the war he escaped to Argentina, and was captured by the Israelis, who brought him to Jerusalem to stand trial for his war crimes. I had very mixed feelings as I witnessed the proceedings. On the one hand I felt extreme anger about what had occurred. On the other hand I felt like a passive bystander. I was in the courtroom almost every day, but I didn't let myself get emotionally involved. I kept saying to myself: "Be calm. Let them be brought to trial and let it all be brought to the attention of the Israeli public." Everything that was recounted there I had experienced for myself; there was nothing new for me to hear. I was only angry that it would take such a long time for the murderers to be sentenced — if they were sentenced at all. It stirred deep feelings of hatred and anger to realize that such an unimpressive, ordinary person could have brought about such death, destruction, and suffering.

Only much later did I grasp how important for history it is to record all details and to write down witnesses' statements, word for word. The witnesses do not live forever, and the following generations must also learn of their fate, their suffering. In addition, this trial was an important event for Israeli society. Those who had been living in Palestine during the Holocaust had the opportunity to learn what had happened to their fellow Jews during this time in Europe. This trial was an important step in the acceptance of the survivors into Israeli society.

In the early 1960s I returned to school. My professional career, after all, called for an academic education, which the war had prevented me from pursuing. So, alongside my work at the Customs Authority, I studied economics and public administration at the Hebrew University's Givat Ram campus. After twenty years of work with the Customs Authority, from 1947 to 1966, having reached the position of acting director general for customs affairs, I decided that I should end my career there. The work had been extremely interesting, not least because it had involved me in the Brussels Customs Treaty, for which I represented Israel together with the customs director. This was the first time in history that Israel was admitted to the United Nations Customs Cooperation Council.

At the beginning of 1967, Sharef, who had in the meantime risen to the post of minister of industry and trade, approached me with the request to reorganize the Ministry of Trade. Since the establishment of the state, the foremost task of this ministry had been to take care of food supplies. Questions about import and export were still in their infancy, and if the economy was to be promoted, the structure of the ministry had to be completely revamped. New industries had to be developed, built up, and established in the country. I recommended investing in high-technology industries and others that were not based on the availability of raw materials but on making use of human resources and ingenuity — design, art, and literature, for example. Within two months I had prepared the new infrastructure. But then the Six Day War broke out, and I had to put my plans on hold for a short time.

The Six Day War was the third war between Israel and its Arab neighbors. In less than a week during June 1967, Israel defeated the armies of Egypt, Jordan, and Syria. The outcome of the war resulted in Israel's control of the Sinai Peninsula, the Golan Heights, and the West Bank of the Jordan River. The war was a watershed in the history of the Arab-Israeli conflict, and its political repercussions are with us to this day. Peace initiatives that have been made, and are still in progress, revolve around the land-for-peace issue.

Immediately following the war in mid-June, I resumed my work and converted my plans into action.

The new organization had a considerable impact on the existing economy. We had to lay off for an extended period a few hundred employees who had worked as inspectors, and take on economics experts, engineers, and scientific staff advisors in their place. Apart from this we set up a research and development fund in order to build up Israel's high-tech industry. The difficulties with which we had to cope were really unbelievable. For example, we started to promote the electronics industry in the country, which at the time consisted of only a single small company run by two young engineers in Haifa. Another fledgling industry started to develop following the French embargo on arms exports to Israel in the wake of the Six Day War: Israel's defense industry.

My interest in promoting industries related to design, art, and literature that would have an impact on Israeli society was prompted by the model of Denmark. At the time, the Danes were successfully exporting not only their home furnishings, but an entire cultural lifestyle. I was sure that Israel could develop and market its own unique culturally influenced products.

With regard to literature, I had already made contact with the international publishing world during my tenure with the Customs Authority. In 1963 the mayor of Jerusalem approached me with a request: He wanted to hold a book fair in Jerusalem, but was having serious problems with the Customs Authority about the books and the need for import licenses. I used my position and ensured that books intended for an exhibition could be imported without customs and licenses, so that the fair could be organized with as few bureaucratic obstacles as possible. The book fair was to make an important contribution to the cosmopolitan nature of our city. At that time, Israelis did not travel abroad as frequently as they do today. The book fair offered them a window onto the international literary and publishing scene. What was more, it also opened a venue for the Israeli literary community to become exposed to international publishing and translation opportunities.

Years later, when I was active in the Ministry of Industry and Trade, I introduced the necessary measures and created the economic infrastructure for Israel's book-publishing industry. For this purpose the Publishing and Printing Committee was organized, which invited professionals from all over the world to provide the industry with the necessary know-how to do business. As one of this committee's founding members, I became deeply involved in the book fair, but at that point I would never have dreamed I would one day be its director. The publishing industry was well suited to the land and the people who had produced the Bible — the biggest best-seller of all time.

But books were not the only thing that interested me. I was also drawn to industries such as architecture and the plastic arts, where design, beauty, and imagination were the reigning forces. Electronic technology interested me because it was based on intellectual potential and not on raw materials. The book industry, however, had an important advantage, namely, export possibilities, if the books were good and translated into other languages or captured on celluloid. Realizing the immense opportunities that a thriving film industry could offer the country by creating jobs for talented people, I devoted much of my time to establishing the Israel Film Center. I arranged to set up labs, import equipment, offer financial incentives to attract foreign productions, and allow local talent to be trained on the job by important international filmmakers. I encountered tough opposition from the country's old-fashioned leaders. "What, in God's name," I was asked, "do we need with 'cinema'?" I argued that if done properly, the films not only could present Israeli culture abroad, but also would bring foreign currency into the country.

True, Israel's film industry is still not one of the world's foremost, but it has become an important part of the Israeli economy. It creates jobs and offers creative people an avenue of expression. Up until 1967 the film industry was not a serious enterprise in Israel, and hardly anyone had anything to do with the movies. But soon after, new film studios were built, foreign productions were being shot here, and the first color film laboratory came into existence in 1968. The facility was imported from the United States and Great Britain.

The film industry moved forward and continued to develop. In the beginning, foreign producers brought mainly westerns to Israel. Films with Tony Curtis and Sally Kellermann were shot in the Negev, which after all is not very different from the deserts of Mexico or Texas. It was funny, though, to see young Israelis dressed as bandits, galloping through the Negev on horseback. Even film stars such as Richard Boone and Gregory Peck couldn't change this. We often said jokingly that now there are not only spaghetti westerns but also matzo-dumpling westerns!

I had not originally intended to be so intensively involved with the film industry. But then the 1973 Yom Kippur War intervened, and my life changed direction again.

For me the Yom Kippur War conjures up feelings of anxiety, alarm, and uncertainty on the family front. In Israel we learn to hide our emotions. No great fuss is made over army service or war injuries — as I learned when I was wounded by shrapnel during the War of Independence in the battle for Haifa. But in truth my wife and I suffered horrendous days during the Yom Kippur War when we heard that our son's unit had been decimated.

I was in Tel Aviv on a visit with close friends whose son, a pilot, had been shot down over Syria during the fighting, and we met there General Ezer Weizmann, Israel's current president. I had no idea of our son's whereabouts, whether he was alive or wounded. When I asked Weizmann what was happening to the 14th Tank Division, he answered: "The 14th Division? Wiped out." No words exist to describe my feelings at that moment. But I tried to keep my composure and gave an evasive answer when he asked why I was interested in that particular unit.

We later learned that our son had survived, and shortly after receiving the good news, I managed, through a quirky turn of events, to meet with him in the Sinai. I myself had been mobilized in Jerusalem, and was engaged in organizing supplies for the civilian population. I received a call from a friend who was the military spokesman at the time. He told me that a group of Americans, among them my friend Marvin Josephson, who later played an important role in my life, wished to visit Sinai with a group of journalists. Marvin wanted to get up-to-date information on the events in Israel, and the journalists, naturally, wanted to report directly from the battlefield. Would I be interested in accompanying the group? I immediately said yes — not least because I hoped to meet my son on this trip. I drove to Tel Aviv and met Marvin and the journalists at the Hilton Hotel. We actually should have all continued on together in one bus, but since I had my own mission, I demanded that a private car be allocated for Marvin and me with a driver. Before leaving I bought chocolates, cigarettes, and sweets in the hotel, and ordered twenty-five packed lunches to ensure that I would have sufficient provisions for a breakfast with my son and his fellow soldiers. In response to Marvin's puzzled look, I told him of my intention. He thought I was a little crazy, since in those days it was almost impossible to find anyone near the Suez Canal, especially if you didn't know where the person was posted.

We finally drove out of Tel Aviv at 2 A.M. It was a very long drive to the Suez. Immediately after crossing the canal we came to a road junction, where the left turn led to Ismailia and the right to Suez. No one knew the way. I insisted that we take the left to Ismailia, because I knew that the 14th Division was fighting under General Ariel Sharon, somewhere in the vicinity of Ismailia. We drove into the desert through indescribable chaos left there by the fighting. I didn't know how in the world we'd find my son near here. But even when my companions became agitated and wanted to turn back, I ordered the driver to press on toward Ismailia. I was overcome with a kind of premonition. It can't be explained rationally. We passed a military command post, then a helicopter. Finally, we seemed to have reached the end of the battle line, and could go no further. But then a truck came toward us, and I asked the driver about the

14th Division. Truck drivers always know things. "Go straight ahead, turn left, and then again straight ahead," he shouted at us from his window. There was hardly a soldier in sight anymore, only a few tanks stood abandoned in the desert sand. The driver became agitated and refused to go any further. I shouted at him like a total fool and begged him to continue driving, until we arrived at what had been an Egyptian position, from which only hours earlier rockets had been launched. In the meantime, an Israeli unit had been posted there. We drove among the Israeli vehicles and soldiers, all the time straight ahead, to the front line. I wanted to come as close as possible to the battlefront itself.

We wended our way through the desert, passing in between military vehicles, until we reached the end of the military road where only a few tanks stood in a semi circle in the sand. Knowing neither which unit this was, nor whether it was my son's, I went on instinct. I shouted at a soldier who was cleaning his machine gun, "Where is Oded Birger?" He answered, "The first tank, there, in front." And then my son, who had been lying on the ground with a blanket over his head to protect himself from a swarm of flies, heard my voice. Convinced he was dreaming, he lifted his head and then saw me. As he ran toward me, we could both hardly believe that I had found him in this confusion of tanks, prisoners of war, and Israeli soldiers. In defiance of all the bad omens, we were now able to have our picnic in the desert. One could call it stubbornness, but I believe it was precisely this strong will and obstinacy that had made it possible for me to survive the hell of the camps.

After I visited my son, my friend General Haim Bar-Lev took the time to explain to me, using aerial photographs, precisely where the Israeli tanks were positioned and how the battle had been fought. When I asked why he was telling me all this — after all, I was not a war expert — he simply said, "Zev, your son fought there."

This was the same son who prompted me to make a wise and honest decision with regard to my career and contribution to the country. In 1977, I gave up my activities in the Ministry of Industry and Trade — to the surprise of many. As acting director general of this ministry, I was responsible for foreign trade and price controls. There were many economic problems in Israel at the time, and the financial situation was a disaster. One day I came home and found my younger son in front of the television. He was studying geology then, but was just back from army service and was sitting in the living room, dirty boots and all. I joined him and together we watched an interview with the finance minister. Suddenly Oded asked, "Listen, don't you know what can be done with the economy?" I told him what suggestions I had and described my ideas to him.

"Okay, so why don't you do it?" was his response.

"Do you really believe that the Finance Minister always does what I say?"

He just replied, "Then what are you doing there?" and went to his room to study.

I was stunned by his blunt reply, but the more I thought about it, the more I had to give him his due. After about an hour I went to his room and said, "I have decided to leave the government."

Without raising his head he said, "Very good." The next morning I went to the minister in charge, Haim Bar-Lev, and told him about my decision to leave government.

At first Haim did not want to believe me when I said I wanted to leave my job, and asked me whether I would consider a promotion. When I said no, he looked at me in complete amazement. I was giving up a professional career for an unknown future without any social security. But I was too disappointed at not having sufficient influence on the country's economic policies, and felt I was working toward something I didn't truly believe in.

It was very awkward to leave the government exactly at this point in time, since Israel was close to the elections and Yitzhak Rabin, who was prime minister at the time, asked me to postpone my resignation until after the elections. I explained to him that my career in the ministry had not been of a political nature, and that I didn't really see any connection with the elections. I related to him the incident with my son that had led to my decision. Though I had agreed to wait with my announcement, the news became known even before the elections, due to an indiscretion, and my planned resignation drew some attention in the media. Thus, I resigned as planned, before the elections took place.

I still had no idea what I would do after taking my leave. It became very difficult, if not entirely impossible, to find a position in Israel. In my position in the Customs Authority and the Ministry of Trade, I had had contacts with many companies that had presented this or that petition to the ministry. It would now have been impossible — in terms of business ethics — to take on a position in an Israeli business. It was important for me to have a "cooling-off" phase abroad, so that I could later take my time looking for a job in Israel.

I had written about my planned career decision to many friends, one of whom was Marvin Josephson, head of the ICM (International Creative Management) Agency in the United States. Marvin and I were good friends, and I admired him as a clever man, a smart businessperson, and a reliable friend. I had often suggested to him in jest that he should come to Israel, that we could use a man like him in the government. In reply he had always proposed that I come to ICM— but this time he said it in earnest. He now repeated the offer. Thus began my work with ICM, which sent me to Paris for three years.

From 1977 to 1980, I headed ICM's film marketing department in Paris, where productions were initiated and their financing made possible by the presale of films that were already at the screenplay stage. The Louis Malle film *Atlantic City*, for example, which came from our marketing house, even won an Oscar. After my return to Israel I was appointed by the minister of education to be head of the film department at the National Council of the Arts. I served as the chairman of the committee for films of artistic merit. Our fund enabled us to support many interesting projects. I regard the establishment of the Jerusalem Film School in the late 1980s as one of the most important ventures I initiated and brought to fruition, despite tremendous opposition from the Tel Aviv establishment. Today the school is an important "trademark" of Israel, and its graduates have brought home many prizes from international festivals.

It was also at that time that my close cooperation and friendship with Teddy Kollek, the mayor of Jerusalem, began. I had known Teddy for quite a while, from the days of the Ben-Gurion government, and also through mutual friends who had been active in Aliya Bet. In 1981, Teddy approached me with a request of a totally different nature, phoning me in Paris. The Jerusalem Book Fair was enmeshed in severe difficulties — important figures had gradually withdrawn from the organization, and the crisis in Lebanon had had a catastrophic effect on international attendance. Kollek wanted to revive the fair and rebuild the publishing contacts abroad. He turned to me because he knew I was familiar with the publishing world from my time in the Ministry of Trade and in Paris, and he also wanted my wife, who had set up a voluntary children's dental aid project, and me to remain in Jerusalem. Anyone who knows him knows Teddy's inimitable powers of persuasion: He can make a request in such a charming manner, hardly anyone has the heart to refuse. I allowed myself to be persuaded to organize the Jerusalem International Book Fair — but for one time only. But things took a different course.

The fair was at first a kind of "family reunion" of friends and publishers who knew each other. We had to make the event more significant and more attractive to the public. This was not supposed to be just a cultural event, but also a profitable venture in business terms. For this purpose we had to somehow distinguish ourselves from other fairs of this kind. A good publishing friend, Esther Margolis, the head of Newmarket Press in New York, came up with an original idea: an Editorial Fellowship Program. This program was intended to offer young publishing people and editors possibilities for advancement as well as an international meeting ground. I decided to implement Esther's idea, and it really took off. An international network of young publishing people was born. Today this project encompasses more than 150 members worldwide. It promotes the flow of literature and culture between countries and brings a breath of fresh air to the international publishing scene. It took some time before we found financially strong sponsors, but more and more publishers were of the opinion that this was a worthwhile project to support and could become an important and integral part of the publishing world. For my seventieth birthday I received a file with letters from over 100 editors who described to me how important the Editorial Fellowship Program had been for their career.

A prominent publisher, who has regularly taken part in the fair since its inception, said to me just recently, "You know, Zev, I like coming again and again to the Jerusalem Book Fair to recharge my batteries — good conversations about literature are hard to come by."

When I asked him why he liked the Jerusalem Book Fair in particular, he answered: "It is big enough to be really businesslike, but also small enough to stay human."

Together with Teddy Kollek, I also worked hard to have the Jerusalem Fairs and Conventions Bureau set up in Jerusalem. We wanted Jerusalem to become an internationally recognized center for business and the arts. I worked by his side as a "one-dollar-a-year man" in order to promote tourism and industry in the city. With this goal in mind, we also established the International Judaica Fair, the Puppet Theater Festival, the Philosophical Encounters, and the Festival for Early Music. The years working with Teddy were fruitful beyond compare; his achievements in generating the cultural development of Jerusalem cannot be appreciated enough.

We had a common desire to make Jerusalem an international meeting point, where a lively cultural exchange between people and cultures could take place, creating a venue for tolerance and peace. These principles played an important role in the founding of the Adam Institute for Education Towards Democracy. This organization was initiated by Teddy Kollek after the murder of Emil Grünzweig. Grünzweig was a peace activist who was murdered during a demonstration in the late 1980s by a hand grenade thrown by right-wing extremists. This was, in effect, the first political murder in Israel since the establishment of the state.

Jerusalem is a city built on hilltops. And on the different hilltops live Jews, Christians, Muslims, Armenians, and many others. Everyone should be allowed to live according to his or her beliefs and with mutual respect and tolerance for others; only in this way can people exist in harmony. This was always my goal in all the projects that I was able to implement with the support of Teddy Kollek. I hope that in the future such goals will also determine the political and cultural life of our country.

EPILOGUE

When I returned to Kaufering with my sons in 1995, it was springtime, the sun was shining, and the birds struck up their seasonal song. Inevitably, I recalled the same setting fifty years earlier. Everything had been so unreal during that spring, so absurd. And now?

I looked across at my sons, who were following the memorial service, their faces grave. No, this was not absurd. I was now here with my family. I was one of the few survivors of the men's camp in Kaufering VII. Where were the others? When I was about to say the Kaddish, the prayer for the dead, my voice failed me for the first time in my life. I could not bring forth a sound. The scenes of the camp once again flashed before me in all their horror. It was as if I were standing among all the dead, the Musselmen, the typhus-stricken, as well as my dying father and my brother who bade me farewell. Images that I had long since forgotten, erased from my memory, were reawakened. I felt as if I were standing by my father's grave and that the Kaddish, which I was supposed to be saying for all the camp victims, should be said only for him, my brother, my mother, and those who were close to me. With a broken voice choked with tears, I finally said the prayer for the dead, with my sons supporting me. We embraced each other, and I had the feeling that they had experienced some of the horror with me.

The theme of the memorial service was "Nevertheless—Yes to Life." This was also my motto when I decided on a new start in Israel. Life would once again have to start from the beginning. After the atrocities I had experienced, I wanted not only to live but also to make a difference — by building the State of Israel, together with my friends and fellow survivors, with and for my family, which after such a long time was finally a real family again.

I looked at my sons and thought about how my wife and I, both survivors of once-large Jewish families, had had to start in Israel from scratch. Our sons were born, and as they got older they began to ask about their family. Why don't we have any uncles? What is a cousin? How can one explain to a five-year-old boy that he no longer has a grandfather or an uncle because they were killed, for the crime of being born Jews? Our sons grew up, got married, and started their own families. And so we are now a family with many grandchildren, uncles, aunts, grandfathers, grandmothers, and cousins. When we all get together on Friday evenings for dinner, there is barely enough space at the table, but there is an abundance of noise, love, and joy.

I am fortunate that our sons and their families are carrying on the values of Trudi's and my parents. Words such as love, warmth, friendship, responsibility, and tolerance are not empty words in their families. They are responsible and loving in their role as educators, but also in their duty toward their country. This is the only proper answer to the Holocaust: We cannot undo what has been done, but we can prevent it from happening again — in whatever form. For this reason, I owed it to my sons and my family, as well as to all those who did not survive the camps, to tell my story.